BUILDINGS & LANDSCAPES

JOURNAL OF THE VERNACULAR ARCHITECTURE FORUM
VOLUME 17 | NUMBER 1 | SPRING 2010

Buildings & Landscapes (ISSN 1936-0886) is published twice a year in the spring and fall by the University of Minnesota Press, 111 Third Avenue South, Suite 290, Minneapolis, MN 55401-2520. http://www.upress.umn.edu

Published in cooperation with the Vernacular Architecture Forum (VAF). Members of the VAF receive the journal as one of the benefits of membership. For further information about membership contact Gabrielle Lanier, VAF Secretary, Vernacular Architecture Forum, P. O. Box 1511, Harrisonburg, VA, 22803-1511, or visit us on the Web at http://www.vernaculararchitectureforum.org.

Postmaster: Send address changes to *Buildings & Landscapes*, University of Minnesota Press, 111 Third Avenue South, Suite 290, Minneapolis, MN 55401-2520.

Manuscript submissions should be prepared to conform to the *Chicago Manual of Style*. Contributors agree that manuscripts submitted to *Buildings & Landscapes* will not be submitted for publication elsewhere while under review by the journal. Please feel free to direct any inquiries to either editor via e-mail: Marta Gutman, Associate Professor of Architecture, The Bernard and Anne Spitzer School of Architecture, The City College of New York, 141 Convent Avenue, New York, NY 10031, mgutman@ccny.cuny.edu; Louis P. Nelson, Associate Professor of Architectural History, School of Architecture, Campbell Hall, University of Virginia, Charlottesville, VA 22904-4122, Lnelson@virginia.edu.

Address subscription orders, changes of address, and business correspondence (including requests for permission and advertising orders) to *Buildings & Landscapes*, University of Minnesota Press, 111 Third Avenue South, Suite 290, Minneapolis, MN 55401-2520.

Subscriptions: Regular rates, U.S.A.: individuals, 1 year, $60; libraries, 1 year, $125. Other countries add $5 for each year's subscription. Checks should be made payable to the University of Minnesota Press. For back issues contact the Vernacular Architecture Forum. *Buildings & Landscapes* is a benefit of membership in the Vernacular Architecture Forum. *Buildings & Landscapes* is available online through Project MUSE, http://muse.jhu.edu, and JSTOR, http://jstor.org.

THE VERNACULAR ARCHITECTURE FORUM
is the premier organization in the United States studying ordinary buildings and landscapes. Established in 1979–80 to promote the appreciation of and scholarship on vernacular structures, it is an interdisciplinary organization composed of scholars from many fields, including history, architectural history, geography, anthropology, sociology, landscape history, preservation, and material culture studies. Since its founding, the VAF has played a major role in the academic study and preservation of common buildings. The VAF holds an annual meeting, publishes a newsletter and a journal, and maintains a Web site.

BUILDINGS & LANDSCAPES

JOURNAL OF THE VERNACULAR ARCHITECTURE FORUM
VOLUME 17 | NUMBER 1 | SPRING 2010

MARTA GUTMAN AND LOUIS P. NELSON

Editors' Introduction

In a mid-September public statement, former president Jimmy Carter claimed, "an overwhelming portion of the intensely demonstrated animosity toward President Barack Obama is based on the fact that he is a black man." Obama has declined to engage the issue publicly. More recently, investigations into Michelle Obama's ancestry revealed that she is descended from both enslaved black and free white southerners. She, too, has declined to comment. The very public nature of these events recalls the much larger debate about the role of both personal and national identity in political formation. Carter's comments focused on white resentment against black advancement, a view that reflected his political maturation during the struggle against Jim Crow. President Obama had previously offered a more nuanced and multiracial view of race relations in his popularly lauded March 2008 speech, in which he called on Americans to transcend the "racial stalemate" of recent decades. If Obama's speech was hailed by some as "post-race," Carter's comment signals that the politics of identity are still very much in play in American politics. In many ways, the essays in this volume offer a scholarly perspective on that debate. Although each argument frames it differently, the politics of identity stand at or near the center of all of them.

The volume opens with Edwin Dobb's keynote from the most recent VAF annual meeting in Butte, Montana, as this edition's *Viewpoint* essay. By seeing Butte through the eyes of the *vernaculus* (Latin root for "native"), Dobb offers a beautifully complex study of Butte and its close relationship with personal and collective identity. This complexity is amplified as he reminds us to consider the multiplicities of perspective that undermine the drive toward any single view on a place. He points out for his readers how natives

of a place can have vested in themselves a deep longing for the past of that place. Desire, he tells us, is a powerful drive that shapes both the way we see a place and influences what it is that we see. This feeling of longing highlights the interdependence of place and identity. He closes by arguing that if the city secures its identity solely in a particular view of the past, the city will die. The Lady of the Rockies—the huge statue of the Virgin Mary that overlooks the town—may then become a witness to a wake. But if the city's identity expands to include a broader view of its own past, it might open to a broader view of possible futures. As did earlier generations, new communities will enter in and make Butte their own—a different Butte, as the town becomes a palimpsest of personal memories and collective identity.

The close alignment between buildings and identity politics is more explicitly realized in two of the articles that follow. Pamela Simpson and Travis Nygard write about the presentation and representation of Native Americans in the corn palaces of the early twentieth-century Upper Midwest. They use two distinct modes: the evocation of Native cultures through the iconographic associations of Native Americans with corn through the nineteenth century (Hiawatha being only the most popular), and the physical presence of native peoples in the parades and celebrations associated with the opening of the corn palaces. In these, the politics of representation and inclusion challenge us to wonder about agency and power over identity formation. Does the act of publicly reifying one's own ethnicity mean a welcome embrace of that presentation? Not necessarily. In the second iteration, they introduce Crow painter Oscar Howe's work: the annual murals in the Mitchell, South Dakota, corn palace. These images highlight the multivalent realities of representation. His Origin of Corn series, for example, could be read as pitting Longfellow's Hiawatha against a Dakota legend. Annmarie Adams's article on the Weston Havens House in Berkeley, California, explores the intersection of sexual identity and architecture by testing the boundaries of queer theory. While the building, designed by architect Harwell Hamilton Harris between 1939 and 1941, was designed for a man presumed by many to be gay, Adams centers her use of queer theory not so much in explicit sexual identity as in the study of "whatever is at odds with the normal, the legitimate, the dominant," to quote David Halperin. Adams uses the ambiguity of a hidden badminton court to examine the reality of public and private, seclusion and exposure, in the life of early twentieth-century gays. Both the Simpson/Nygard and the Adams articles engage quite directly the role of identity politics in interpreting buildings and landscapes.

If these articles engage the politics of personal identity, the two remaining articles deal with the politics of national identity, in a manner not unlike Dobb's work on Butte but at different scales. Allen Miller's work foregrounds the role of lighthouses as the first major federal works projects after the American Revolution. In an era when many questioned the role of a powerful federal state, Miller argues, lighthouses were both pragmatic necessities for the support of national commerce, and subtle symbols of a cohesive federal identity. He highlights the example of the Cape Henry lighthouse on the Chesapeake Bay as the first of a series of lighthouses that shared a common form and common function, both pragmatic and symbolic. He argues that these early lighthouses are now understood largely in local isolation, but in the decades after the War, they emerged as among the first material manifestations of a cohesive federal state. Lillian Makeda also engages the federal government, but at a later era and in the guise of the National Park Service. Her article on the privately owned roadside establishment called the Lion Farm, immediately adjacent to Petrified Forest National Park, is an excellent case study of the Park Service's struggle to engineer a particular understanding of a national public by deciding who from that public could shape the architectural experience of a national park. In a well-understood contest,

the essay pits a particular public interest against the private interests of small-scale entrepreneurs. The essay forces us to ask who plays the lead in building a "public" identity. Together with the essays that address identity politics more explicitly, these essays suggest that we are not yet postidentity, that the role of architecture in shaping who we think we are is still a critical issue in scholarship on the built environment.

Before we conclude, let us introduce two structural changes we intend to make to future editions of *Buildings & Landscapes*. The first is our intention to begin publishing reader responses to content in the journal by dedicating a page or two to letters to the editors. If you take exception to an article or find it particularly helpful or just think that something important was left unsaid, please let us know. We will publish your comments in the next edition. It is our intent that this will foster even greater dialogue among our readers about the meanings of vernacular places. The second change affects our book reviews. In an effort to add reviews of Web sites and exhibitions and to cover more books than has been the case in the past, we are hoping to substantially increase the number of reviews in each edition, which means they will be a bit shorter. But because *Buildings & Landscapes* is the premier scholarly venue dedicated to vernacular architecture, Andrew argued, and we agreed, that more comprehensive coverage is essential. So beginning with the next edition, please expect to find more book reviews.

As always, we hope you find this edition of the journal compelling and inspiring. If so, please write to tell us. If you find it maddening, infuriating, or frustrating, tell us. We look forward to your thoughts.

EDWIN DOBB

Viewpoint: Location, Occupation, Juxtaposition, Interpenetration

Notes on an Erotics of the Mining City

To Orient

Most of us are animated by what might be called the cosmological impulse—a reflexive tendency to orient ourselves with respect to space and time. It's so deep-seated that we usually don't think about it. On a mundane level, the impulse manifests itself in a variety of ways, depending on circumstance. In cities such as New York, where I lived for ten years before moving back to Butte, people usually ask, "What do you do?" But when I returned to Butte, the first questions almost always concerned parish, neighborhood, and family connections. Kinship trumped all other ways in which one might "place" someone else. *Oh, I went to school with your mother.* Or: *Your dad worked with my uncle.* Or: *My cousin is married to your cousin.* There was nothing better than that: discovering that the stranger you just met is in fact a relative. Your name was your calling card. *I don't know who you are until I know who you're related to and what part of town you come from.*

This was a map that you developed unconsciously and which stayed with you. And you can still find it today. When I met John T. Shea, my neighbor, now a dear friend, he stood on North Main Street and, while pointing to empty lots in both directions, recited the names of people long dead who once lived and worked in buildings that were razed years ago—residences, bars, grocery stores, boarding houses. All within the shadow of the Mountain Con Mine, where his father worked, a mile below the surface across the street from the family home. John T. says that he and his buddies stole the bottles that miners placed outside the second-story windows of the Mullan, the biggest of the boarding houses in

the neighborhood. That was the first sign of his knack for climbing, which served him well later when he became an ironworker building those very headframes. His labor is embodied—and memorialized—in several of the thirteen headframes that have survived and that today stand as the most iconic structures in town. As I listened to John, the now-empty lots and silent streets came alive, ever so briefly. Much of what was here is gone, but not to those who lived here before.

"I was born to this," John T. Shea says. And by that he means both the place and the life it has offered. The Mining City. Mining. The mines. This is the voice of a native, of course. Native: one born or reared in a particular place. The Latin form of which, of course, is vernaculus, which literally means *native to a certain place and time.* Contrasted with what's uncharacteristic, foreign—originating elsewhere. Some people are born to a particular place and time; others are not. They are outsiders. Visitors. Butte has a reputation for friendliness toward outsiders. And it is well deserved. But part of Butte's maddening complexity, and contributing to both its persistence and its fatality, is that it is one of the hardest clubs in the world to join. You can go a long time without noticing this demarcation, but once you do recognize it, suddenly the town seems impenetrable—and inscrutable. It's a place you cannot enter under your own power. To convert from outsider to insider, you must be invited, sponsored—adopted. It helps to have an Irish surname.

So here we are at the Mother Lode Theater, a group of outsiders, united by an interest in other people's local realities, visitors to a place that's especially resistant to such endeavors, that's stubbornly, even combatively tribal in its intent not to reveal its inner workings. I believe that's called a dilemma. And I include myself, by the way, among the outsiders, as well as in the problematic endeavor. At least in part. I'm a vernaculus, certainly, and so in every significant respect a product of the specific place that was Butte at a certain time—from 1950 to 1968. That's the "this" I was born to. But at the first opportunity, and with not one iota of regret or grief, I fled my hometown. More than that, I tried to forget the place altogether, tried to erase all ties and traces. I was driven by the conviction that my identity was mine to invent as I saw fit. Renouncing the known world, in my view, was the only way to start that quixotic endeavor. For twenty-five years, I put more and more distance, both emotional and geographical, between where I came from and where I imagined I was going. And I succeeded to such a degree that when I returned in 1993 (by then having realized that I'd left a good part of my identity behind), Butte was foreign to me. Not entirely so, to be sure. It had become an amalgam of the familiar and the unfamiliar.

The experience was something like partially forgetting a language that I was once fluent in, that I had once been immersed in and conversant with, though not conscious of. So I set out on a quest to re-read the Mining City. This required patience and lots of time, watching and listening, trying to be alert to the moments when the place, as it is now, spoke to me. It required that I pay special attention to the occasions when the local, the vernacular, without losing anything that made it so, revealed how it fit into the larger vocabulary of human existence, where the topical intersects the universal.

From my foursquare cottage, located across North Main Street from the Lexington Mine, I've been watching and listening for seventeen years, almost as long as my first life here. Though far from finished, I'm now in a position to suggest a simple but fruitful method that outsiders can use to decipher the Mining City, to make it at least temporarily scrutable.

Erotics of Place

I can imagine someone objecting to what I've just said: "Aren't you making too much of this insider–outsider distinction? After all, we're not cultural anthropologists. We study the built environment. We're not trying to join a club; we just want to examine the clubhouse, or whatever might be left of it." What persuades me that there's more to this argument than straw is the term "built environment," which, please forgive me, is an unfortunate choice of words, both aesthetically and, more important, semantically. I recently learned that the term was chosen as an alternative to the pretensions and formality of the word "architecture," but the result is eerily passive—indeed, seems to stress the absence of agency. Not only is no one home, home somehow came into existence on its own.

I'm exaggerating to make a point, of course. Surely everyone who uses the term "built environment" knows that he or she is referring to a set of human artifacts. Someone constructed the buildings; someone fashioned the natural world into landscapes, then remade the landscapes, then remade them yet again. And these actions were taken under certain historical, cultural, social, and economic circumstances. No news there. But words matter. So does clarity of thought. The danger in the term "built environment" is that the more it is employed, the easier it becomes to devalue the builder. What I propose is the reverse: I want to highlight agency, I want to bring to the foreground how the things that hold our attention today came into existence. And of the many ways one might go about that—in terms of social factors, of economic forces, or of something similar—I further propose that we adopt a more primal approach, looking at Butte through the lens of human desire.

I don't mean desire in the narrow psychological sense—"Crazed by Avarice, Lust and Rum, Butte, thy name is Delirium," wrote Warren G. Davenport in 1909—although all that is included. I have in mind the larger aggregate of life-preserving instincts. Everything we need and—a crucial distinction for human beings, everything we believe we need—to survive, flourish, multiply, elaborate, make more complex. In other words, Eros. The imperative that drives us all. The hard flame that burns within every living thing, from vanishingly small microbes to ecosystems of continental proportion. Viewed from this perspective, the Mining City can be seen as one of the planet's erogenous zones: a place, at least for awhile, of exceptional desirability, a place that invited and aroused extraordinary passion.

Little of which is obvious today. The human energy that once made this one of the most dynamic places in America has long since dissipated. Instead, the desire that is sometime most in evidence today is longing—longing for the Butte of yesteryear, of particular yesteryears. Indeed, much of the current romance of Butte is the doomed romance of the ruin, of traces and whispers and ghostly things that aren't readily graspable. History, we must remember, is the study of the invisible, a refusal to let bygones be bygones, the academic equivalent of an endless wake.

The wonder is that so much can be divined from traces, whispers, and ghostly things, that the lost, via its vestiges, its echoes, can be recovered, not as something visible and tangible, of course, but as something imagined—an imaginary restoration, however, that's based on evidence that is itself available to the eyes, fingertips, ears. That's the genius, the joy, of the architectural detective work that the people in this room do. And this is a location where the vernacular detective's brand of inquiry can be richly rewarding. Ever a place of extremes, Butte remains fascinating for its rawness, its explicitness. Much that might be hidden or erased elsewhere is on display here. More than that, it is celebrated. In Butte, there will be times when you find yourself, as the poet Wallace Stevens wrote, "in the presence of extraordinary actuality."

As a rough framework for an erotics of that actuality I'll briefly describe four ways that buildings and landscapes are configured in Butte: location, occupation, juxtaposition, interpenetration. These configurations certainly aren't unique to Butte, but in many instances they possess unique characteristics or assume uniquely revealing forms.

To Locate

How is it that people and things came to be located here? Why was Summit Valley transformed into a compelling destination, a locus of intense, sustained desire? What stirred people to such a frenzy?

As Dick Gibson's scientific introduction in the field guide explains, the enticement was the Boulder Batholith. (Though I doubt Dick realized he was composing the first chapter of an erotic history of Butte. Who knew that geology could be so sexy?) The Boulder Batholith is the reason that virtually overnight Butte was transformed from a ramshackle mining camp into an industrial metropolis, the only camp in the West where that happened. It's the reason Butte endured all the ups and downs, the reason mining continues today. It's also the reason we've assembled in this room. Beneath this very building lies one of the richest ore bodies in the world. That's why a drama of epic proportions played out on this small, out-of-the-way stage.

Tens of millions of years ago, immense lenses of magma rose upward from the earth's interior, eventually solidifying into one body of granite— a batholith, or rock from below. As the magma cooled, cracks formed that, in turn, filled with water and bits of molten copper, silver, gold, and molybdenum, which also solidified. Erosion followed, exposing the mineral-rich fractures, or at least making them accessible from the surface. The minerals were deposited in zones, roughly circular in shape, with silver, lead, zinc, and manganese more prevalent in the outer rings and copper dominating the center. One of the mines located in the central district was Marcus Daly's Anaconda. There, in 1882, Daly's men struck an unusually large vein of copper. From that moment on, geology was destiny.

The Age of Electricity had gotten under way only a few years before, with the invention of the telephone and electric light. America's appetite for copper, by far the best-known electrical conductor, suddenly became insatiable. Like an immense red sun, Butte drew all manner of human beings into its orbit: Irish and Cornish at first. Then immigrants from eastern and southern Europe, from Scandinavia, from Mexico and China, from Indian reservations in Montana, from all over the country. "No Smoking" signs in the Butte mines were written in at least sixteen different languages.

Most residents lived on the slope that forms the northern end of Summit Valley, known locally as the Hill (although in time the town also spread southward, out onto the valley floor, an area called the Flat, or Flats). On the Hill, and especially on the east side of the Hill, people constructed neighborhoods, all defined by ethnicity and religion, near the underground mines, enabling miners to walk to and from work. The development of the original part of the city, in other words, took place directly atop the ore body—a fateful turn whose profound consequences no one foresaw, and which continue to reverberate to this day. (I'll return to this later.)

To Occupy

What took place in Butte from the early 1880s until about 1920 was not a gentle process. Not a

relatively benign agricultural transformation, by which first nature was converted into the second nature of farms and ranches. Here was an occupation of staggering speed, intensity, and disruption. America, in its appetite for copper and other minerals, took possession of Butte via highly aggressive, large-scale resource extraction. In Butte, the Industrial Revolution collided with the romance of the West, giving birth to something that might be called "frontier industrialism" (Figure 1). The result was a mining metropolis. An urban–industrial island. Butte becomes comprehensible only when viewed through this lens, as a city in every respect but size—the Pittsburgh of the West (Figure 2).

The population in 1880 was about 3,300. Within twenty years it jumped to 40,000. By 1920, it reached nearly 90,000. At the peak, from 1915 to 1918, as many as 16,000 men worked in mining. And work is the key to everything here. This was a place that worked hard, a place that was worked hard, then reworked and reworked, contributing mightily to the industrialization of America. From the late 1880s through World War I, Butte produced more copper than any other place in the world, including one-third to one-half of the U.S. supply. From the early struggles over ownership and influence, one corporation emerged to take control of all the operations—the Anaconda Copper Mining Company, the fifth-largest industrial entity in the world by 1920.[1]

Eventually, some 10,000 miles of workings—shafts thousands of feet deep, drifts that radiate out under the city—were developed beneath an area of only five square miles. Butte was two cities: one above ground, another below. And once you crossed the threshold, descending into the underground realm, you could never be sure you'd return. During the early decades, the place that billed itself "the richest hill on Earth" was also the most dangerous in the world. Injury was commonplace, death routine. The costliest accident took place in 1917. The Granite Mountain–Speculator Fire, when 168 men died in what still stands as the worst hard rock mining disaster in U.S. history. Anyone wishing to plumb the significance of Butte should make a pilgrimage to the Granite Mountain Memorial (Figure 3). It's

Figure 1. Postcard of Butte, circa 1920s

Figure 2. Main Street. Photograph by Arthur Rothstein, Farm Security Administration, 1939.

Figure 3. Granite Mountain Mine Headframe. Photograph by Dick Gibson.

hallowed ground. From the overlook you can see the Granite Mountain headframe. You can also see an example of Butte's rawness, its lack of shame—a mining landscape that will remain as it is. Former historic preservation officer Mark Reavis says that the entire history of mining is visible from that spot, and if you look closely, you'll realize that he's right. Industrial archaeologist Pat Malone calls it "the industrial sublime." And it surely possesses a kind of haunted, ravished beauty.

It is also a place where we are reminded that Eros was always at risk here, always engaged in a potentially lethal dance with Thanatos, the forces of death.

That dance took a decidedly different turn with the excavation of the Berkeley Pit, the most extreme example of occupation, yielding a permanent disfigurement of the landscape. When pit mining replaced underground mining (the last closed in the mid-'70s), the cost of taking possession of Butte's mineral resources was no longer measured in terms of physical injury and death but in damage to land, water, and air, as well as in the accompanying social and psychological toll of displacement.

To Juxtapose

During Butte's heyday, the sights and sounds of mining—of industry and labor—were ever-present. This was a very noisy place: Ore trains constantly coming and going. Cages and skips rising and descending on the headframes. Sheave wheels squealing as they turn. Mine whistles blowing. Because of the mines' omnipresence, deciphering traces and vestiges today

Figure 4. Alice Mine Dump, after reclamation. Photograph by Dick Gibson.

often entails interpreting juxtapositions of urban fragments and environmental reclamation sites. One of those juxtapositions is located in my neighborhood—Walkerville, a separate municipality within Butte that was home to many of the town's Cornish residents (Figure 4). It is the Alice Dump, capped and revegetated. Located on the outer ring of the mineralized district, the Alice was a silver mine, both the original underground operation and the pit excavation that succeeded it.

Urban and industrial elements sitting side by side is common to most industrial communities. But in Butte the juxtapositions can be unusually intimate and telling, starting with the most dramatic instance of all—the proximity of the Berkeley Pit, the largest contaminated manmade

body of water in the country, to the old business–residential core (Figure 5). This is the defining juxtaposition of the Mining City, cause and consequence joined together. Most Americans who benefited from the copper and other minerals that came out of the Butte district were, and are, far removed from the environmental legacy of large-scale industrialized mining. Not Butte. Indeed, the town must live with—must literally live next door to—the legacy from here on out.

But living and working have always butted up against each other in Butte. No one could escape the primary truth of the place: everyone depended on mining, which, in turn, depended on the miners forging a common purpose from all their differences. This was the Gibraltar of unionism, the birthplace of the Western Federation of Miners and the Women's Protective Union. During the early decades of the town, almost every type of worker was organized, including newsboys, waitresses, maids, and theater ushers. Although it took a while, Butte came to understand that it did its best, both as a place to live and a place to work, when it stood together. And never did it stand together with more conviction or effectiveness than during the 1934 strike, a direct result of FDR's encouragement of organized labor. The solidarity that developed then—and which paralleled what was taking place in other industrial towns around the country—fostered social stability, intergenerational continuity, community cohesion. That's when the Mining City developed the story that it continues to tell itself today—that it can withstand all hardships, all downturns, that it will endure. What it didn't realize is that it had inadvertently provided a much-needed counterpoint to the dominant myth of the West—the primacy of the individual, the notion of solitary self-sufficiency.

Here's a wonderful example of the domestic and industrial realms sitting side by side (Figure 6). Notice the child: she is playing in a landscape dominated by mining. This was routine, and no one I knew growing up here—in the '50s and '60s—considered it a form of impoverishment. Quite the opposite. We found the place to be endlessly rich and stimulating, a thousand times more interesting than the fakery of a Disneyland. If you were curious enough, and tough enough, childhood conferred a kind of passport that enabled you to move, often unnoticed, between the very different realms of the Mining City.

One of my early playgrounds was a stretch of mine waste bordered by a stream that ran orange and yellow. We called it Shit Creek. Today, it's the site of the concentrator, where ore bearing small amounts of copper and molybdenum is prepared for smelting. Another playground, when I visited my older cousins on the Hill, was the Steward Mine. I'm not talking about the idle yard one sees today (Figure 7). We played there while the mine operated. It helped to be lucky. It also helped to be able to run fast and scale fences quickly. I could cite more examples: The red light district, for instance, was located only a couple blocks

Figure 5. Berkeley Pit. Courtesy NASA.

Figure 6. Steward Mine. Photograph by Arthur Rothstein, Farm Security Administration, 1939.

from my high school (Figure 8). We routinely walked past working brothels to get to the stores and soda fountains uptown. Or maybe to one of the bars that served teenagers—another way in which what might be considered transgressive elsewhere was tolerated in Butte.

Figure 7. Steward engine room. Photograph by Jet Lowe.

Figure 8. Former brothel. Photograph by Dick Gibson.

To Interpenetrate

Because the occupation of Butte via industrialized mining persisted for an unusually long time, juxtaposition often became interpenetration, sometimes with unfortunate results. The ethnic neighborhoods on the east end of the Hill—Finntown, Meaderville, and so on, which contributed to the mosaic of architectural styles here—were destroyed to make way for the Berkeley Pit.

In the social realm, by contrast, interpenetration sometimes led to a beneficial mingling of ethnic or religious groups, or economic classes. One place where that happened, and that still exists today, is the M&M, which Jack Kerouac referred to as his "ideal bar" (though I suspect that Kerouac, a hard drinker all his life, managed

to locate an "ideal bar" in every town he visited). The old M&M was a place where ironworkers and miners might sit next to lawyers and bankers, the usual divisions temporarily erased.

Juxtaposition had always invited interpenetration. Placement led to displacement. What was written could be erased, if it served the work, the life. We sometimes forget that the destruction of the neighborhoods started not with the Berkeley Pit, but earlier, with the gradual encroachment of the Kelley Mine complex into the signature Irish enclave Dublin Gulch. Central to the work here was reworking, rebuilding, reinventing. When my neighbor John T. Shea maps the Mining City for me, he includes when this or that building burned down or was replaced by something else. Some of the surviving headframes, for example, were first constructed at other mines, then disassembled, transferred, and reassembled. And how many of the older houses in Butte contain timber and pipe that the company thought it owned but somehow lost track of?

Everywhere you look, you find signs of this opportunistic, sometimes ruthless dynamism. Here are examples of the interpenetration of mining and civil society, the burial of Holy Savior School (Figure 9) and the Columbia Gardens (Figure 10), Butte's versions of Coney Island and Central Park, joined together and once valued just as much. Here is a building whose purpose has been radically reworked over the decades (Figure 11), from swanky social club for the elite of Butte to union headquarters to, perhaps, an Irish cultural and historical center.

One of the most imaginative new kinds of interpenetration is a vision of reconciliation that was developed back in the late '70s and early '80s, when the heroic period of mining ended and the environmental era began. Fred Quivik and Mark Reavis played pivotal roles in developing this ingenious approach, which takes into account the unusual degree and range of juxtaposition in Butte by attempting to combine historic preservation, environmental reclamation, and economic development. This is another aspect of the buildings and landscapes here that deserves consideration. For now, I'll mention only two of my favorite examples: the engine room at the Belmont Mine converted into a senior citizen center and the recent conversion of the Original Mine Yard into the main stage of the National Folk Festival (Figure 12). I like these because they're inspired cases of "usable history."

The Granite Mountain Memorial is also an example of usable history, not only as a reminder of the human cost of industrialized hard rock mining but as a stunning example of what an industrial landscape looks like. When the past and the present interpenetrate, there's a danger that reclamation will become a form of erasure, of inadvertently or deliberately induced amnesia. That won't happen in this part of the perservation/reclamation/development corridor. So far, Butte has done a good job of resisting the Disneyfication of its industrial history. But the temptation will always be with us.

Beyond Native, Beyond Nativism

My final example of interpenetration is the Lady of the Rockies (Figure 13), the nine-story steel statue that stands atop the East Ridge, some 3,500 feet above the valley floor. More than anything else in recent history, the construction of the Lady of the Rockies is a manifestation of the town's inimitable character, its quirky vitality, its refusal to quit. In some respects, the Lady is the ultimate in vernacular structures. It emerged wholly from within the community, in the absence of guile or calculation, all the labor volunteered, all the materials and money donated by locals. A few years earlier, after a hundred years of virtually continuous operation, the mines had closed down entirely. Something that no one imagined possible had in fact happened. At a time when the town had every reason to despair, it came up with this extravagant act, the collective elaboration of one man's modest vow to erect a small Madonna-like statue in gratitude for his wife's having survived a serious illness. The Lady can be described in many ways, but the one I find most illuminating is this: the interpenetration of work and the spiritual life of the community. Profane and sacred mingling together. It was work by other means and in an entirely different context, one in which traditional skills and solidarity were essential but in which the wages were measured in moral, emotional, and spiritual terms.

Figure 9. Holy Savior School being buried. Courtesy the *Montana Standard.*

Figure 10. Columbia Gardens, surrounded by mine waste. Courtesy the *Montana Standard.*

Figure 11. Butte Miners Union No. 1. Courtesy Butte–Silver Bow Public Archives.

The story Butte tells itself about the Lady is that she gazed across the valley, looking over the weary city, the ravaged landscape, and said, "This town needs help." Ever since the lights went on, in late 1985, she's been seen as a protector, a beneficent maternal figure that, among other things, harkens back to all the women over the years who mended individuals, families, whole neighborhoods rent asunder by mining. A kind

Figure 12. Original Mine. Photograph by Dick Gibson.

of collective prayer for mercy. But sometimes when I see the statue standing above the Mining City, I can't escape the impression that what I'm watching is a wake, a wake that's been going on for twenty-five years, sustained in large part by reclamation money and other federal funds related to environmental cleanup. A wake for the Mining City.

I think it's time we brought the wake to an end. The Mining City—and bear in mind, I mean a very specific place and time—isn't coming back. Whatever Butte's future may hold, it won't look like that, not ever again. All our talk about the spirit of the place enduring, which is true enough (and which I believe as well), can also be a form of whistling in the dark, of not mustering up the courage to look into the casket and at long last

acknowledge what has happened. The Mining City is dead. Kiss it goodbye. The only way it lives on is in remembrance, a source of inspiration. But it's not a place where the living can reside. We can draw from it, we can dwell on it, *but we can't dwell in it.*

So where do we go from here? I'd like to suggest a new story for the Lady, once she's free from standing vigil over the Mining City. A story that, in my view, is more fitting for the times we live in. When now I look at those open arms, hands turned outward, I prefer to think that instead of a gesture of consolation directed toward the people of Butte—"Come to me, I'll comfort you"—what I'm seeing is a gesture of invitation to the world beyond Butte. "Come, we need new blood, new energy, new ideas." The Lady as a beacon. Butte's

Figure 13. Lady of the Rockies. Photograph by Dick Gibson.

own Statue of Liberty. But let's call it the Statue of Liberation—liberation from a past that we honor, certainly, and that we're damned lucky to have flowing through our veins, but a past that we've finally put to rest.

This might not seem so sacrilegious if we recognize that the "past" that we speak so reverentially about today doesn't reach much further back than living memory. It, too, is a specific locality, circumscribed in time and by historical circumstance. Starting, at the earliest, in the 1920s and ending in, say, the 1960s, or perhaps the mid-1970s, when the last of the underground mines closed. But another Butte existed before that. And it was a radically different place. That town, from 1880 to 1920, was made up almost entirely of visitors. Natives came later. That's something we tend to forget when we're thinking—or not thinking clearly—about the past. New places are always first occupied by foreigners. They aren't born to this, they're born to something else, then come to this—or, more precisely, create this. If we wish to privilege a certain group by virtue of how early they lived somewhere, we should compose odes to foreigners, build monuments to outsiders. And the foreigners who stay, who make a place their own, shaping its unique local character, including the built environment, are precisely the people who eventually produce the special individuals we call natives—all those little vernacula that represent the promise of any community. In other words, their children, and their children's children. In 1900, 88 percent of the population was under twenty-five years old. Picture that: nine-tenths of Butte's 40,000 residents (more people than live here today) were younger than twenty-five. And you can be sure they weren't arguing over who was or was not an authentic Buttician.

That was the period of the "wide open town" that Myron Brinig described in his novel of the same name. That was the Butte of "Butte, thy name is Delirium." The Butte about which ur-feminist and bohemian Mary MacLane posed the devilish question, "Where is its equal?" That era of the town's history, I believe, should also inspire us today, along with the long middle period of social stability and intergenerational continuity that usually governs remembrance. We need a new period of immigration. A new kind of interpenetration—the present no longer clinging desperately to what was but instead embracing what might be. Is there a risk in this? Without question. Allowing outsiders to join our club may change us, and it will almost certainly alter this place. But the alternatives, I'm afraid, are prolonged stagnation or, worse, the gradual transformation of a once uncommonly vibrant town into a cemetery, life pitched amid gravestones—aging, increasingly insular natives polishing memorials to nativism. The final defeat of Eros.

Again and again I hear the fear expressed that Butte might go the way of, say, Bozeman, striking a devil's bargain that will result in the town's losing what makes it distinctive. But we must not forget that we have something Bozeman and other much-coveted towns in western Montana do not—an immense environmental mess right on our doorstep. That curse, it turns out, is also a charm: more precisely, a shield, and one that is more protective than the Lady. The vernacular reality of Butte includes an industrial and mining landscape that functions as a firewall, thwarting the weak of mind and spirit, the unimaginative, the affluent second-homers and recreational thrill-seekers who owe allegiance to no particular place or time, the disappointed, disoriented souls who come looking for the Montana they've drooled over in travel brochures and glossy magazines, not realizing that when they enter Butte they leave Montana behind.

For the past seventeen years I've watched people come and go. In my experience, those who fall in love with this odd, broken, often forbidding place, those in whom Butte arouses passion and loyalty and a desire to stay, are exactly the newcomers—the new blood, the new erotic force—we need most. Imagine the vitality and creativity that might flourish here were we to follow the example of the Lady on the mountain, opening *our* arms to them, adopting them and making room for their children, thereby inaugurating a new era of wide-openness.

NOTE

1. Mary Murphy, *Mining Cultures: Men, Women, and Leisure in Butte, 1914–1941* (Urbana: University of Illinois Press, 1997).

ALLEN S. MILLER

"The Lighthouse Top I See"

*Lighthouses as Instruments and Manifestations
of State Building in the Early Republic*

Oh! dream of joy! is this indeed
The lighthouse top I see?
Is this the hill? is this the kirk?
Is this my own country?
  —Samuel Taylor Coleridge,
  The Rime of the Ancient Mariner

The joy of the occasion notwithstanding, the cold morning light of a New York Wednesday, the fourth of March 1789, exposed the truly ethereal nature of the federal government and of the American state itself. Soldiers fired celebratory volleys and musicians played ceremonial fanfares, but the United States Congress had nowhere to hold its first meeting. Its borrowed home was still undergoing renovation and expansion. With a sarcastic wit, Representative Frederick Muhlenberg described the recently re-dubbed Federal Hall as "elegant and well design[ed]—for a Trap."[1] Weeks would pass before the Senate or House could establish a quorum. Although citizens had cast their votes to elect George Washington as president, the government could not convene electors and validate the results until that quorum was established. The executive-to-be would not be sworn into office—there was no oath of office as of yet—or even arrive in New York for more than a month. The executive departments of the Treasury, War, and State would not be established for another five months. A system of federal courts would not be established until the following fall. Although the general organizational structure of the new government was defined by the recently ratified Constitution, for those convening in New York, and for all citizens of the new United

States of America, the federal state was merely a state of mind existing only on paper or in the imagination. Any evidence of its existence as a unified, sovereign entity was difficult to find in New York or anywhere else across the rest of the country. As a result, the elected and appointed officials gathering in the new federal capital over the weeks, months, and years to come would work diligently to create political institutions possessing widely acknowledged authority (as a demonstration of unity) and a recognizable state presence (the essence of sovereignty). Unfortunately, how they should go about doing so was largely undetermined.

One of the few agreed-upon avenues for establishing authority and presence was federal regulation of commerce. Four of the first five items of legislation considered by the House of Representatives dealt with commerce, and more than 40 percent of all legislation introduced and considered during the first session of Congress dealt with this subject. Although most of these bills sought to promote American political and economic unity and sovereignty through a coordinated system of duties and imposts, one particular bill supported a far more tangible projection of federal presence: lighthouses. The initial mention of lighthouses in Congress occurred barely a month after its first meeting, during debate on the Tonnage Act (HR-5) on April 4, 1789. In part, this discussion occurred because the transfer of power for levying and collecting duties on shipping from state to federal authorities also removed the mechanism for funding lighthouses at the local level.[2] Notwithstanding this financial reality, other factors played a role in the delegation to federal authorities of responsibility for operation, maintenance, and propagation of lighthouses. These were the regulation of commerce and promotion of public safety, two imperatives that concurrently nurtured unity and sovereignty. As such, lighthouses were important early instruments and manifestations of an expanding federal authority and presence. These factors, as well as the process by which that presence was negotiated and constructed, shaped the form and directed the location of these structures after *The Lighthouse Act* (HR-12) was passed on August 1789.[3]

Five factors exerted influence in this regard. The first was lighthouses' utilitarian function as a crucial aid to navigation. Another was their role as an instrument in the federal government's efforts to weave local and regional trade networks into a cohesive national economy. Very much a consequence of that objective was a new federal perspective that viewed lighthouses not as isolated, individual structures, but as parts of a systematized network of standard elements. Fourth, as prominent manifestations of the state, lighthouses needed to be unambiguous representations of its capacity and competence, its credibility and stability—as well as a promise of its longevity. Furthermore, the buildings needed to do all this in a manner consistent with republican ideology. Fifth, the assertion of federal authority over existing lighthouses and the subsequent multiplication of them were not without controversy; in dealing with this reality, federal efforts to avoid controversy, and the processes of negotiation, accommodation, and compromise that determined federal policy had a profound effect on the design and construction of lighthouses. By studying these early federal structures and the forces that exerted an influence on their form and location, one gains a greater understanding of the challenges, methods, and results of early state-building initiatives. Before beginning an analysis of the buildings themselves, it is necessary to understand the circumstances that influenced federal actions.

To enhance the likelihood of ratification, the Constitution was necessarily vague with regards to the location of specific boundaries between federal and state authority. Generally, the areas of governance and policy least suited to fragmentary action—for example, security, foreign relations, and the regulation of commerce—had been willingly allocated by the several states to the new central government. In other areas, where the advantage of consolidated federal action was debatable, the locus of power continued to be unresolved. Furthermore, even when there was more or less unanimous agreement on the aptness of federal authority, there remained the potential for state or public objections based on how, or even if, that authority would be implemented and exercised. For example, were any and all methods of regulating commerce acceptable? Clearly they were not, but the Constitution gave no guidance as to how such distinctions were to be made. In fact, when it came to the process of governance, the Constitution was sorely lacking in both specific answers and general guidelines, being rather a rough sketch that some historians have characterized as no more than "controversial presumption, inference, and supposition."[4]

From the perspective of officeholders, equally problematic with this lack of a clear understanding of the scope and means of exercising federal authority was the accompanying absence of a consensus on the precise goal of state building. Beyond the most generic definition of state building as the establishment of a unified, sovereign polity through the creation of processes and institutions in accordance with shared republican values, the specific goal of American state building was ill-defined. What exactly did a republican government look and act like? No modern state (or even an ancient one) warranted imitation. This was Madison's conclusion in his "Of Ancient and Modern Confederacies," which he completed in 1787 as part of his preparation for the Constitutional Convention. Moreover, there was no precise blueprint or thoroughly articulated description to follow in the Constitution, or elsewhere. Under these circumstances, how was one to convert an ideological vision of a republic into a unified, sovereign state that effectively exercised and accurately manifested that ideology? The failed attempt to establish a sustainable relationship between the states under the Articles of Confederation eloquently testified to the absence of an answer. Even after ratification of the Constitution, there was no consensus as to what the goal of federal officials should be: it was understood only to be something more than a loose confederation but less than a centralized nation-state. Rather, a more specific sense of how the state should look and act began to coalesce only as the new government initiated its policies and actions—and it would continue to evolve for decades.

If all this were not enough, unity and sovereignty would need to be established within an incredibly complex political environment. A population of anxious individuals and what George Washington called "so many distinct communities"—well-established institutions—already exercised power in a number of overlapping domains.[5] When it came to lighthouses, five types of "communities" were involved. The first was composed of members of the general populace who expressed their interest both collectively and as individuals—for example, as landowners or neighbors of existing and potential lighthouse sites, or as seamen, fishermen, or shipowners. The second category was composed of interest groups: for example, those who shared a political ideology, or groups (such as the Chamber of Commerce of the City of New York and the Boston Marine Society) with shared economic interests. Third, and obviously, one of the most powerful communities was the group of preexisting states, each with its own particular array of interests and priorities, some common, some unique. Fourth, the federal government was itself a community and—perhaps most ambivalent of all—was endeavoring to simultaneously represent its own specific interest as well as the collective interests of others. Fifth were foreign countries and the international community, whose interests were many and varied, ranging from sympathetic to hostile. These groups tended to have differing, often conflicting perspectives, and the process of crafting a unifying solution in the face of those divergent views—by definition the goal of state building—was extremely challenging. Furthermore, because the membership of communities evolved dynamically, their interests changed almost continuously. Where and how the machinery of federal governance would be

assembled within this landscape of existing powers was far from obvious. The extent of circumstantial complexity and dynamism meant that improvisation and flexibility would be essential. Federal officeholders needed to avoid imposing on existing power, to sidestep controversy or conflict, and to gently manage confrontation, when it did occur, through a process of accommodation and compromise.

One other factor further narrowed the federal path through the political landscape. The ratification of the Constitution notwithstanding, fear of centralized power continued to haunt most Americans. Having fought to free themselves from the bonds of metropolitan authority, the several states and their citizens remained anxious, jealous of their rights and skeptical of—if not actually opposed to—the reimposition of any similar authority. This being the case, the reaction to any misstep by federal authorities was greeted with exaggerated disfavor. Some historians have suggested that the new government, aware of this sensitivity, endeavored to be "light and inconspicuous," to operate on the verge of public consciousness.[6] Certainly, given the reality of circumstances, the federal government needed to be cautious. However, because the essence of unity and sovereignty were acknowledged federal authority and recognizable state presence, any effort to remain truly inconspicuous would be wholly counterproductive. During the earliest years of the republic, federal officials found success allaying public fears by embracing a number of policy initiatives that created a more distributed, less centralized authority and presence. Not only did that embrace directly address the fear of centralized power, but it also promoted contact of a more empathetic kind between citizens and the federal state. The sum of these circumstances reveals that the federal government adopted a two-pronged approach intended to address the concerns of both individual and collective constituencies. On the one hand, federal officials improvised as unforeseen institutional obstacles arose, changing course where possible or adopting a process of accommodation and compromise where controversy or conflict was unavoidable. At the same time, they created diffuse instruments and manifestations

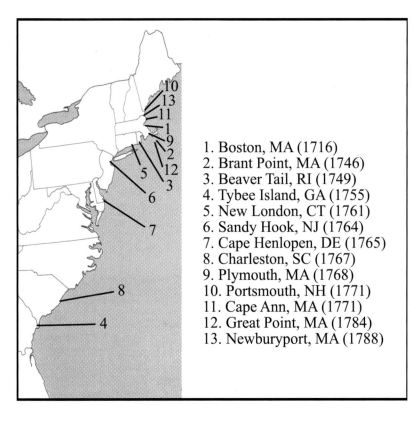

1. Boston, MA (1716)
2. Brant Point, MA (1746)
3. Beaver Tail, RI (1749)
4. Tybee Island, GA (1755)
5. New London, CT (1761)
6. Sandy Hook, NJ (1764)
7. Cape Henlopen, DE (1765)
8. Charleston, SC (1767)
9. Plymouth, MA (1768)
10. Portsmouth, NH (1771)
11. Cape Ann, MA (1771)
12. Great Point, MA (1784)
13. Newburyport, MA (1788)

Figure 1. Colonial Lighthouses Federalized by Act of Congress, 1789. Data from D. Alan Stevenson, *The World's Lighthouses before 1820* (London: Oxford University Press, 1959), 173, 176–78. Map by the author.

of the federal state that were far from inconspicuous, but still subtle.

This is certainly demonstrated by the early development of authority through the federalization and ensuing propagation of lighthouses. Many Americans recognized not only that this extensive network of navigational aids was an important means of regulating commerce among the states and with foreign countries, but also that their imposing yet benevolent presence along the coast was an appropriate means of projecting the presence and power of the new federal state. This being the case, the design of these lighthouses stemmed not just from their functional role as aids to navigation, but also descended directly from the process of state building itself. The function, form, location, construction techniques and materials, and operational technology of federal lighthouses all bear the fingerprints of policymakers, because decisions about those issues were as much a reflection of strategic concerns about state building and commercial policy as they were of environmental, economic, and operational factors. Put simply, lighthouses of the period looked the way they did not only because of the navigational imperative,

but also as a result of the economic, ideological, and political factors influencing those who chartered, designed, and built them.

By 1789, thirteen lighthouses erected by various former colonies were scattered along the coast from Portsmouth (New Hampshire) to Tybee Island (near Savannah, Georgia) (Figure 1). The placement of these facilities had been determined solely on the basis of independent local action without any larger systematic view. They were built to mark the entrance of a particular harbor as a means of promoting and protecting local commerce. As a result, long stretches of desolate coastline remained unmarked. Of greater concern to many people, even where lighthouses existed, they operated with varying degrees of reliability. Many lighthouses had been damaged during the Revolutionary War or had fallen into disrepair during a prolonged period of diminished maritime activity that produced proportionately less "light money" for upkeep.[7] At least five lighthouses, at Plymouth (Massachusetts), Cape Henlopen (Delaware), Tybee Island (Georgia), Boston (Massachusetts), and Sandy Hook (New Jersey) were in disrepair or even extinguished for varying periods of time. This general deterioration of lighthouses occurred within the larger context of indebtedness among the several states, a situation that would eventually lead to the assumption of state war debts by the federal government. Although three states (Massachusetts, Virginia, and North Carolina) were ambitious enough to have additional lighthouses planned or under construction (Portland, Cape Henry, and Bald Head respectively), some general remediation was urgently required. Various constituencies demanded action to create a more reliable system that would protect public safety and property, as well as regulate commerce.[8]

On August 7, 1789, federal authorities complied by signing into law *An Act for the Establishment and Support of Light-Houses, Beacons, Buoys, and Public Piers* [HR-12]. Under the act, states had the option of ceding the title and jurisdiction for lighthouses and the land upon which they stood to federal authorities in return for the operation and upkeep of these critical facilities. The act also specified the construction of a lighthouse on Cape Henry at the mouth of Chesapeake Bay, a project begun more than a decade before, but never completed. As the individual states moved to make the necessary cessions, lighthouses and those persons chartered with their operation quickly became an important federal institution, a visible representation of the federal state. As the National Park Service has written, "The high level of attention given to lighthouses . . . was tied directly to [*both* the nation's] need for commerce and its desire to . . . instill confidence in ship captains as well as foreign governments, symbolically implying that the United States was a responsible world power worthy of due recognition."[9]

Of all the American lighthouses predating 1789, the one on Sandy Hook at the eastern approach to New York harbor would prove to be the most influential on the design and construction of those built by the federal government. Erected in 1764 and still in use today, this octagonal stone tower capped by a domed copper and iron lantern served as the design prototype for many major North American lighthouses well into the nineteenth century. This resulted from the central roles played by two influential New Yorkers. When he drafted the request for proposals for the first federal lighthouse, Secretary of the Treasury Alexander Hamilton described a building very similar to the lighthouse on Sandy Hook—a structure he must have known from his work as a New York commercial entrepreneur. In responding to the request, New York architect John McComb used the same model. In addition to dimensions and cost estimates for his own lighthouse proposals, his memorandum books contain detailed notes on Isaac Conro's original design for and cost of the Sandy Hook lighthouse. McComb's proposals all followed Conro's design with great fealty (Figures 2 and 3). Contractors who built other lighthouses also adopted this scheme. Even when they departed from it in favor of a modified conical form (as opposed to the original's octagonal footprint), they closely adhered to Conro's general ratios of the tower's height and width at its top and bottom, and of the thickness of its walls at given elevations.[10] Builders and officeholders embraced this approach—shaped by local experience—as a

Figure 2. Nathaniel R. Ewan, "Sandy Hook Lighthouse," photograph, Historic American Building Survey, May 10, 1937 (Washington DC: Library of Congress), call number HABS NJ,13-SANHO-2.

Figure 3. Cape Henry Lighthouse, Cape Henry, Virginia. Photograph by the author, January 13, 2008.

reliable means of accurately estimating costs and minimizing objections to untried designs during a period when proposals that even hinted at controversy were shunned. Because the Sandy Hook Lighthouse was recognized as a thoroughly successful execution of the form, the emulation of this tried and true model was an obvious means for avoiding controversy. In this respect, Sandy

Hook's design met the requirements of political and strategic expediency.

With increasing frequency, federal authorities located lighthouses in remote, exposed locations, thereby bringing even greater attention to issues of structural integrity and cost of maintenance that required construction to incorporate the best practices and most durable materials available. This insistence on high-quality construction had the fortuitous effect of fulfilling the mandate to create manifestations of federal credibility and stability, as well as a convincing omen of federal longevity. Finally, the unadorned, highly functional form of the lighthouse on Sandy Hook was consistent with the demand that manifestations of federal power exist in harmony with an ideology that rejected any indication of monarchical symbols or "superfluities."[11]

To encourage its passage, the Lighthouse Act included a provision that "a Light-House shall be erected near the entrance of Chesapeake-Bay." Such a proposal—the first federal works project—was a powerful inducement with more than local appeal. The first whiff of political bacon wafting through the legislative chamber, held an obvious appeal for Virginia's representatives, but it also attracted the support of merchants throughout the Chesapeake region. One Baltimore merchant noted a lighthouse was likely to "gain the Blessings of Thousands" because of its location in the "most wild & dangerous part of the Bay."[12] A lighthouse at Cape Henry, the unnamed but assumed location for the project (where Virginia had previously gathered materials for a lighthouse), would also create a much-needed link in the chain of lighthouses stretching between northern and southern states—in 1789, there were only two lighthouses south of Delaware Bay. It would do a great deal to encourage coastal trade by eliminating the huge gap between the lighthouses at Cape Henlopen (Delaware) and Charleston (South Carolina), thereby promoting the presence of a cohesive state united by the bonds of commerce. Here, at the earliest instance, is evidence of the shift away from an isolated local perspective to a broader systematic one. Moreover, the federal government repeatedly took the initiative to spend money on expanding what was soon viewed as the network of lighthouses, thereby underscoring their relative importance.

Following passage of the Act, it fell to the Treasury Department to make the Lighthouse Act a functioning reality. Alexander Hamilton spent much of the fall of 1789 collecting information about existing lighthouses, including their condition and operation. On October 1, 1789, he addressed a Treasury Department Circular to all Collectors of Customs requesting information about lighthouses in their respective districts. Two factors led to his choice of these officials as a source of information. One was the fact that these men were familiar with the circumstances since many of them had previously held a similar position in port cities under state authority. The other was the inextricable connection between customs duties—i.e., "light money"—and lighthouses. The replies he received ranged from the explanation that no lighthouses existed in certain areas, to straightforward identification of lights and their keepers, to pleas for urgent repairs and improvements. Collectors of Customs Thomas Randell and William Heyer of New York wrote Hamilton expressing their concern that a recently damaged beacon near Sandy Hook Light was "essential to the safety of such vessels as may find it expedient to come within the Hook at night." That not all of the correspondence came from the Collectors of Customs indicates the close working relationship between these officials, influential local merchants, and concerned groups. For example, on November 11, Hamilton received a letter from attorney Joseph Otis of Barnstable, Massachusetts suggesting a lighthouse in the area "would be the Means of saving many lives." Less than a week later, Capt. Mungo Mackay wrote on behalf of the Boston Marine Society urging the "Reform . . . of this harbor" in regards to navigation. The third week of November brought an extraordinary letter from Norfolk (Virginia) attorney Thomas Newton Jr. containing "estimates . . . of the cost of building a Light House on Cape Henry in Virginia—an account of materials which were placed on the spot for that purpose—and . . . a [draft] of the Light House which was to have been erected."[13]

Shortly after the New Year, Hamilton sent a letter containing a "Report on Light Houses" to the president. It compiled all the information, recommendations, and budgets for lighthouses in states for which Hamilton had information (he had received no information for Georgia or North Carolina). Given their logical connection to the structures, he proposed that lighthouses be supervised by the Collector of Customs nearest to each one and that these officials be empowered to negotiate contracts for supplies and maintenance of the lighthouses subject to recommendation by the Secretary of the Treasury and approval by the President. Hamilton also recommended retaining the existing keepers for the time being (nearly all would eventually be retained long-term).[14] Finally, he presented a state-by-state budget proposal that made it clear that many of these facilities were in disrepair. Although Connecticut and New Hampshire had budgets of only $450 and $217 respectively, New York and Pennsylvania lighthouses required extensive repairs that pushed budgets far higher—to $1,500 and $4,133, respectively. Massachusetts and Virginia had lighthouses in various stages of construction for which funds had to be appropriated. The budget for finishing the partially completed Portland Head Light was a hefty $6,000 and to build the proposed Cape Henry Lighthouse was a gigantic (although strangely precise) $34,076.66 plus $2,000 maintenance per year.[15] This important document is certainly the earliest plan to establish and fund a systematized, geographically distributed federal bureaucracy around federal works projects.

Hamilton's official correspondence for 1790 is littered with scores of references to lighthouses. Merely the number and frequency of these references attest to their importance. The references fall into three categories: the status of contracts for supplies and repairs, the need for cash to pay bills associated with these contracts and the salaries of keepers, and the cession to the federal government of title to and jurisdiction over the land and improvements pertaining to lighthouses. The correspondence relating to contracts was perhaps the most urgent, because the continuous operation of lighthouses with their benefits to public safety and commerce—as

well as their status as visible manifestations of the federal state's viability and credibility—relied directly upon a supply of oil, wicks, and other consumables. The slow, inefficient process for approving contracts created the need for improvisation by keepers and supervisors but eventually gave way to a simplified acquisition process. The need for cash was equally acute. A series of supplemental appropriations was required, and these took time. Even after these appropriations were authorized by Congress, cash had to be found. Again improvisation was the order of the day. When cash was not forthcoming, several Collectors of Customs advanced their own funds, others dipped directly into the sums received from tonnage duties before forwarding them to the Treasury Department, and one unilaterally reduced a lighthouse keeper's salary.[16] The ingenuity of individuals aside, these struggles produced new, more efficient processes that would serve as models for subsequent federal programs for more than two decades.

Along with maintenance and supply came the challenging responsibilities associated with more ambitious lighthouse construction projects. Intended to foster the state building cause, these projects were generally located in remote areas where their presence served to guide mariners between ports rather than to any single port in particular and was only practical when undertaken through the collective effort of various constituencies. The histories of two particular lighthouses, Cape Henry in Virginia and Montauk Point in New York, serve as excellent examples of this evolving process and of the building forms they produced.

Given the Lighthouse Act's explicit authorization to build and pay for a lighthouse at the mouth of Chesapeake Bay, Virginia's extraordinary eagerness to work toward a cession of land is easy to understand. With this situation in mind, Hamilton endeavored to move forward at Cape Henry, relying heavily on Thomas Newton Jr. of Norfolk, whose father enjoyed political and personal connections with Washington, Jefferson, and Madison. Newton's earlier correspondence with the President and Hamilton indicated his familiarity with the project, and Hamilton sought to draw

Figure 4. "Section of the
Cape Henry Lighthouse
as Built, 1792," *The Old
Lighthouse at Cape Henry,
Virginia: An Account of
Early Efforts to Establish a
Lighthouse at the Entrance
to Chesapeake Bay,
1607–1789* (Richmond:
Association for
Preservation of Virginia
Antiquities, 1947).

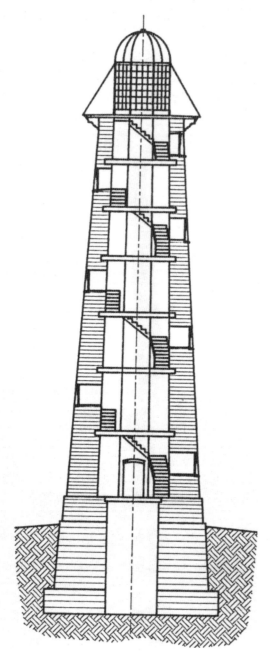

pletely inconsistent with federal strategic objectives, and Hamilton ignored it.

A request for proposals for construction of the lighthouse at Cape Henry was published in numerous newspapers during the fall of 1790. Hamilton included seven responses in his report to the president, dismissing the five highest bids as wholly unacceptable while focusing on those received from John McComb Jr. of New York and Joseph Clarke of Annapolis. Although Clarke's bid was the lowest, his proposal did not meet the letter of the specification. Hamilton's concerns about Cape Henry's exposed location and shifting sands—expressed repeatedly in his earlier correspondence with Newton—were a key to his recommendation. Quite taken by the similarity of McComb's design to the lighthouses at Cape Henlopen and Sandy Hook, Hamilton noted that "the latter . . . has in a great measure been taken as a model." As noted above, McComb's personal journals make it explicitly clear that this was in fact his method for designing and estimating the costs of construction for Cape Henry. Hamilton also pointed out that the lighthouses at Cape Henlopen and Sandy Hook were located in physical environments very similar to that of Cape Henry, and had "borne the test of repeated examination, and the trial of time," essentially validating their standing as examples of best practice.[18]

The new lighthouse's status as the first federal public works project required proven solutions for reasons beyond the need to ensure reliability and control maintenance costs in a remote location. First, by conforming to familiar, admired models, Hamilton sought to avoid the controversy inherent in any innovative approach. Second, these models were acknowledged as incorporating best practices that would reflect positively on the competence and credibility of the state. Third, by building a monumental lighthouse that was likely to stand for centuries, the United States was making a statement about its own stability and intended longevity. Finally, with Sandy Hook standing approximately 145 miles to the north of Cape Henlopen, erecting another lighthouse of a similar design at a virtually equal distance (about 150 miles) to the south was the first step in converting individual lighthouses into a coordinated, systematized federal network.

on this by making Newton his eyes and ears at Cape Henry. In June 1790, Hamilton wrote Newton requesting him to inspect the proposed site and arrange for a survey. The following month, Newton sent a favorable report containing his endorsement of the site, despite its shifting sands, but suggesting that construction of the lighthouse be of wood because "it would take three or four years in all probability to finish one of stone."[17] This particular suggestion was com-

With all this in mind, Hamilton recommended McComb's proposal for a robust tower of solid hewn stone (at $15,200, only 20 percent more expensive than Clarke's less substantial design). Washington concurred, and the contract was let to McComb.[19]

With action now shifting to the coast of Virginia, Newton and McComb became the key actors. Cape Henry, an open expanse of rolling dunes located at the southern juncture of Chesapeake Bay and the Atlantic Ocean, was exposed to the full force of coastal storms. Eighteenth-century drawings and descriptions of the area and photographs from the late nineteenth century all indicate a minimum of vegetation to hold the sand in place, and shifting sand had caused the original construction attempt to be delayed before it was finally abandoned at the onset of the Revolution. Now, as McComb began his work, it quickly became evident that earlier concerns about the relative instability of the ground at Cape Henry were warranted. Writing to Hamilton, Newton observed, "the drifting of the sand is truly vexatious, for in an instant there came down fifty cart loads at least, in the foundation after it was cleaned for laying the stone." Changes needed to be made. Under the circumstances, the government in general (and Hamilton in particular) was wholly dependent on McComb and Newton. Through the summer construction season of 1791 and again the following year, the foundation of the lighthouse would be extended to meet the need for a more substantial structural base. Completed in October 1792, the lighthouse was an important physical manifestation of the state (Figure 4). Although its location was remote in terrestrial terms, it inhabited a distinctly prominent position in the maritime environment, linking the north and south, the new world and old.[20]

As such, Cape Henry was the first of a series of lighthouses erected by the federal government that reshaped Americans' ideas about the primary function of lighthouses (Figure 5). Because their funding and placement during colonial times was determined at the local level, lighthouses were almost always situated near the entrance to a harbor and their significance was always measured in a local context. They were structures intended to lead mariners to an

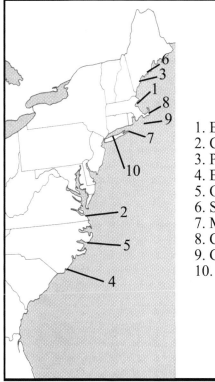

1. Baker's Island, MA (1791)
2. Cape Henry, VA (1791)
3. Portland Head, ME (1791)
4. Bald Head, NC (1794)
5. Ocracoke, NC (1794)
6. Seguin Island, ME (1796)
7. Montauk Point, NY (1796)
8. Cape Cod, MA (1797)
9. Gay Head, MA (1798)
10. Eaton's Neck, NY (1799)

immediate destination not (in many cases) away from a hazard or toward some other distant port. However, federal lighthouses at Cape Henry (1791), Bald Head (North Carolina, 1794), Seguin Island (Maine, 1796), Truro on Cape Cod (Massachusetts, 1797), and at Montauk Point on Long Island (New York, 1796) all set new standards as terrestrially remote navigational landmarks of regional and national significance. This contextual reorientation of lighthouses constitutes critical evidence of deliberate state building. Lighthouses were instruments that would solidify the economic bonds between the several states while enhancing federal standing. On the Outer Banks of North Carolina, lighthouses at Bald Head and Ocracoke Inlet (1794) did much to enhance navigation, commerce, and political unity between north and south. They also extended the network of standardized federal lighthouses at approximately regular intervals along the coast to the south (Table 1). However, because of its strategic importance for both coastal and international commerce, no lighthouse project was more significant than that at Montauk Point.

In the fall of 1791, Assistant Secretary of the Treasury Tench Coxe wrote to the New York

Figure 5. Lighthouses Built Under Federal Authority: 1789–1799. Data from D. Alan Stevenson, *The World's Lighthouses before 1820*, 181. Map by the author.

Table 1: Lighthouses of the Federal Network: Distance to Next Major Lighthouse (north to south)

Montauk Point Light	Sandy Hook Light	Cape Henlopen Light	Cape Henry Light	Ocracoke Inlet Light	Bald Head Light	Charleston Harbor Light	Tybee Island Light
135	145	150	160	170	160	40	

Congressional delegation asking about the value of building a lighthouse at Montauk Point. The Senate directed Aaron Burr (New York), Robert Morris (Pennsylvania), and James Gunn (Georgia) to "consider the expediency of building a light-house on Montauk Point . . . and if they think expedient, to report a bill for that purpose," which they did five days later on March 6, 1792. The Senate promptly passed the bill, and the House subsequently agreed and passed a supplementary funding bill on April 12, 1792.[21] Given its rapid approval, the project seemed to be well on its way, but circumstances soon changed, and it would be more than three years before ground was broken for the lighthouse.

This delay was not the result of disagreement among constituencies as to the desirability of building at Montauk. The speedy passage of the original bill attested to consensus. The Chamber of Commerce of the City of New York had been instrumental in choosing the site of the lighthouse prior to the passage of legislation, and after passage, support came from throughout the northeast. For example, Joseph Anthony, a Philadelphia merchant wrote Coxe an evocative letter in January 1793, proclaiming that "a light on Montague [sic] would be of infinite service" to the people of Long Island and eastern Connecticut, as well as "benefit the trade of Rhode Island and all of Massachusetts." Anthony added that it would "in fact be serviceable to the trade of all the Middle States . . . giving the most universal Relief and Satisfaction." Here is evidence that a lighthouse on Montauk Point would be well situated to foster federal objectives.[22]

Paradoxically, against this background of broad support, the cause of the project's postponement was the intercession of its instigator, Tench Coxe, who expressed concern about restrictions in New York's cession of property for the lighthouse. The state specifically retained its right to enforce state law on the property. This decision may have been more a matter of practicality than an expression of state's rights, for contemporary evidence attests to the sense that Montauk was beyond the reach of the law. Located on the easternmost tip of Long Island, approximately 125 miles from New York City, Montauk was a frontier inhabited by Native Americans and a few people of European descent. Land-based transportation was primitive, so virtually all travel between Montauk and the outside world was waterborne. Twenty miles nearly due north of Montauk, New London (Connecticut) enjoyed cordial but tenuous relations with the settlers of the small island community. The busy port of Sag Harbor was located to the west of Montauk on Long Island, but being twenty miles from Montauk, it endured similar disadvantages of geographic isolation. In fact, the entire southeastern fork of Long Island, a narrow spit of land stretching fifty miles out into the Atlantic Ocean, was not just geographically isolated but sparsely populated (just 1,497 residents in 1790). Although stories that the early eighteenth-century pirate Captain Kidd buried his treasure in Montauk are probably false, the Point and its environs were certainly a strategic haven for those who chose to live outside the law. Montauk's settlers repeatedly suffered at the hands of interlopers who had landed under cover of the Point's high bluffs and then crept up to commit crimes "such as killing their calves, sheep, [and] cattle."[23] With this in mind, the establishment of order and security around and within a federal enclave were prominent in the minds of New York legislators.

Practical considerations notwithstanding, Coxe believed the provisional cession of jurisdiction was inconsistent with both the Enclave Clause of the Constitution and the Lighthouse Act. Attorney General Edmund Randolph was quickly consulted, and although he was noncommittal on the question of constitutionality, he did support Coxe's opinion that the cession fell short of the Act's intent.[24] Although the inconsistency of the cession caused the administration to delay construction of Montauk Light, forces worked to avoid a wider constitutional conflict and to preserve both this specific project and the developing network of lighthouses as a whole. Randolph, engaging in the ultimate act of compromise and accommodation, sidestepped the question of constitutionality by simply ignoring it.[25] The Congress expressed its willingness to accommodate the states by passing new legislation limiting the parameters of the required cessions.[26]

During this period of federal maneuvering, correspondence received by the Treasury Department illustrates the convergence of lighthouses and federal presence in the public mind. For example, in a letter of January 1793, a mariner wrote expressing his concern for safety as well as his national pride: "If the great object is to conduct ships into safety from the Great Atlantic . . . Montauk Light is as necessary as Henlopen or Sandy Hook." It would also contribute to the "growing state of our coastal trade, which I consider as one of the ornamental plumes in the Cap of dame America." Later in the year, as delays persisted, New York City's Collector of Customs Patrick Dennis wrote to Coxe, lamenting:

> Nearly two years ago the Secretary [of the Treasury] requested us of this port if any improvements was wanting. . . . On this request an extra meeting of the Chamber of Commerce was called and their report sent. . . . We hear nothing of it since. Many of the foreigners who come to our port complain to me and say we pay largely to the support of your government and are but badly accommodated with light. . . . This is hurtfull [sic] to my feelings as I know their complaints is too well founded.

Dennis concluded his letter pointing out that progress at Montauk would result in both "the improvement of our navigation as well as the reputation of our government." These examples indicate that by the end of 1793, people saw lighthouses as an expression of the federal state and indicative of its condition.[27]

Although it would be more than a year before Congress passed a new comprehensive Lighthouse Act, it did pass an interim measure on May 12, 1794, thereby allowing a request for proposals for the Montauk project to be issued. Although the federal contracting process ran relatively smoothly by now (once again, John McComb was the successful bidder), the purchase of land for the lighthouse was far more problematic. One reason for this is fairly obvious: the knowledge that the federal government was committed to build on the site prompted the owners to drive a hard bargain. Just as at Cape Henry, the federal government found its fate in the hands of a local representative, in this case Henry Dering, the Collector of Customs in Sag Harbor (New York). Dering tried to wage an uphill battle against the sellers' demands, some of which were met and included in the registered deed, a document that was signed by an astonishing total of fifty-two owners and potential heirs to the property.[28]

Even when the legislative and legal hurdles had been overcome, the difficulties of building in such a remote location were formidable. McComb's 1795 estimate for the project (i.e., his costs versus the price he intended to charge the federal government) reflects the difficulty of construction in such a remote and sparsely populated location. Once again he patterned his proposal after Sandy Hook Light, but in this case, virtually everything required for construction—not just materials, but labor and provisions—had to be brought to Montauk Point from a significant distance. The cost of transporting the stone for the lighthouse to the site was far more than the cost of the material itself—$1,140 versus $780. The cost of provisioning was nearly equal to the cost of labor—$991 (including 500 gallons of rum) versus $1,110. Carts, horses, and oxen, as well as oats and hay, needed to be brought from other locations. Even though the designs of the lighthouses were very similar, McComb estimated that building the lighthouse at Montauk would be nearly 50 percent more expensive than building the one at Cape Henry, and his proposal to the federal government reflected that increase ($15,200 versus $22,300).[29]

It is readily apparent that all these projects were ill suited to local or state (as opposed to federal) control. All were distant from any substantial commercial center, the traditional catalysts for lighthouse construction. All required a legal and managerial commitment, as well as a financial investment that exceeded a municipality's, or even a state's, willingness or ability. Furthermore, there was no incentive for local investment, because the benefits that accrued from any of these projects were regional or national rather than local. In another sense, by providing aid to international trade; by virtue of their location on federal rather than state territory; and by their projection of federal presence beyond national borders, these lighthouses took on the appearance of what might be called external rather than internal improvements.[30] In these circumstances, the importance of structural forms that projected the state's credibility, stability, and ideological identity took on the added role of establishing national sovereignty.

Once construction on Montauk Light had begun, it progressed remarkably quickly. On April 23, 1796, Dering wrote Coxe notifying him that construction had begun and that McComb was "very thorough and acquainted with the work" and had suggested moving the tower farther back from the edge of the bluffs, a suggestion that was rejected. By the beginning of June, McComb had completed the dwelling house and by the end of the month had completed the tower's foundation. With autumn and the end of the construction season quickly approaching, Dering wrote Coxe with palpable excitement that "I . . . would inform you that I saw the posts of the lantern raised and . . . stone work nearly completed . . . I should do injustice to my feelings not to mention that . . . Mr. McComb does his work in a faithful and workmanlike manner." With efforts already underway to secure oil for the lighthouse, on November 18, 1796, Dering sent two separate letters to Coxe. The first stated, "I do hereby certify that I have this day visited the Light House, Oil Vault, and Dwelling House at this place built by Mr. John McComb Jr. from whom I have received the keys of said buildings, which are in every respect completed and finished." The completion of the buildings so noted, the second letter inquires of Coxe when the lamps for the lighthouse would arrive and states that "I

[Dering] shall wish to receive your instructions in lighting the lantern whether the same will be lighted on receipt of the lamps or whether a previous public notice will be expected." Although not yet illuminated, the construction of the Montauk Point lighthouse was finally completed, four years and eight months after Congressional approval (Figure 6).[31]

Yet problems persisted, for just one month later Henry Dering sadly informed Coxe, "I have heard this morning that the vessel in which the oil for the Light House . . . was shipped . . . was drove on shore in the late violent gale of wind," and added "this unfortunately will retard the lighting of the lanthorn [sic]." Dering was not done for there was more bad news to convey: "another and greater difficulty [is] in the glass's blowing out [of the lantern] and breaking—fifteen lights or squares were broken." It would be the following spring before the repairs were completed, more lamps and oil procured, and the lighthouse finally illuminated. Over the winter Dering corresponded in a philosophical mood with Coxe, writing, "It takes some time to get this building under way and many impediments have been thrown at it . . . but I have no doubt of it being of great benefit and usefulness to navigation [for] both vessels from sea and those bound coast wise and will be the means of saving much property and many lives." He also absolved McComb of any blame for the difficulties being encountered, a conclusion Coxe shared upon his review of reports on Montauk and Cape Henry. The test of time has proven their regard for McComb to be well-founded. Of the ten lighthouses built by the federal government during the 1790s, only four of the original towers are still standing today. Three of those—Cape Henry, Montauk Point, and Eaton's Neck (New York)—were built by John McComb Jr.[32]

Visiting Montauk soon after the completion of the lighthouse, Timothy Dwight paints an evocative picture of the new building and its surroundings:

There are four or five English families on this peninsula. These unfortunates are from two to three miles apart, so that each house is a hermitage. One of them has the care of the lighthouse, a structure

A VIEW of The Light House on Mantock Point

eighty feet in height, standing in an elevated situation on a point, distinguished soon after the colonization of this country as a landmark of the first importance. Perhaps no building of this useful kind was ever erected on this side of the Atlantic in a spot where it was more necessary for the preservation of man.[33]

Now, more than two centuries after they were built, these early lighthouses still captivate the observer—although for very different reasons than those Americans found compelling in the 1790s. Americans still respond to their monumentality, but as isolated objects, not as parts of a complex network of navigational aids, or more profoundly as important instruments and manifestations of the burgeoning federal state. Joshua A. Taylor writes, "a national symbol . . . rarely comes about through purely metaphysical promptings. Adopted for immediate and practical purposes, it acquires power as it makes its way through history." That is certainly true,

but history is just as likely to diminish, obscure, or even erase the significance of national symbols as their relative importance as practical objects evolve. When federal lighthouses were first designed and built, they fulfilled a crucial function as aids to navigation. They were conspicuously important. Although the two leading navigational guides of the era, John Norman's *American Pilot*, and Edmund Blunt's more highly regarded and widely used *American Coast Pilot*, occasionally specify the latitude of certain marks, they rely far more often on navigating by dead-reckoning relative to the distance and bearing of visual marks. This method was ubiquitous because, at the time, there was no widely available means of accurately determining longitudinal position. Therefore, for determining one's position, lighthouses were important during the day, and essential at night. Blunt added notes on Montauk Light to his guide within a year of the lighthouse's completion.[34] The obvious functional importance of these structures then—and

Figure 6. Mary McComb, "Montauk Point Lighthouse," 14 1/2 x 21 3/4 in.; watercolor, gouache, ink (New York: New York Historical Society, 1796), 1898.3.

Figure 7. Detail of "Plan Elevation & Section of the Different Buildings Intended to Be Erected at Eaton's Neck on Long Island, NY, 4 August 1799," by John McComb Jr. (New York: New York Historical Society, PR 040, box 5, drawing #85, 1799).

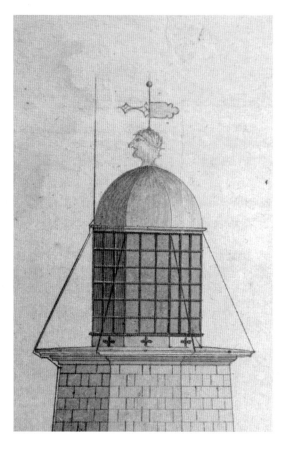

ironically their diminishing practical importance over the recent decades—does a great deal to prove Taylor's hypothesis.[35]

As representations of the state, American lighthouses were designed not only to perform a particular task as aids to navigation, but also to project a visible image consistent with a republican ideology that valued practicality and performance over the visual "superfluities" and flourishes of an authoritarian power. Given these concerns, both the advertisement requesting proposals and the contract for the lighthouse at Cape Henry (the first constructed under federal authority) went into great detail about the materials and form of the building.[36] The foundation and tower were to be constructed of "hewn or hammer dressed stone" in the form of an octagon, with three windows in the eastern face of the building and four in the western one. These windows and the single door were framed with exceedingly simple sills, lintels, and jambs. The interior of the tower was faced with brick and featureless with the exception of a series of semicircular nooks for storing a relatively small quantity

of oil around the chamber inside the entry. Seven flights of wooden stairs ascended to the lantern. The stonework of the tower was to be topped by a platform of wooden joists and planks forming the floor of the lantern and a projecting balcony that allowed the keeper to reach the outside of lantern for cleaning and maintenance. These timbers and planks, inside and out, were covered with copper to reduce the chance of fire. The lantern itself (also octagonal) was constructed of a wrought-iron frame, four uprights of which were anchored to a depth of ten feet in the upper stone work of the tower. The eight sashes, also fabricated from iron, each held twenty-eight panes of glass. The roof of the lantern was a dome formed from an iron hoop and ribs covered with copper sheathing. An iron frame from the top of the lantern to the outer edge of its projecting base supported a brass wire mesh intended to protect the windows from hail and birds attracted to the light at night. This design and its execution are notable for its sturdy, simple, utilitarian character.[37] As such, it followed the example of McComb's proven model at Sandy Hook and expressed the practicality and restraint of the fledgling federal state.

Finally, according to the contract, the lantern would be topped with the lighthouse's only ornamental feature—something akin to the figureheads adorning ships of the era—a "large Copper ventilator . . . to be made in the form of a Man's Head [which] shall be so placed as to be turned by a large Vane which shall be fixed to the spire above it." Some historians have suggested that the head was intended to be a likeness of George Washington. However, the idea of having a likeness of the head-of-state crowning a state building would have been completely antithetical to the conscious avoidance of such iconography in other circumstances. Speaking through his friends in the Virginia Congressional delegation during the debate of a bill creating the United States Mint in 1792, Washington made it clear that he believed the use of the president's image on coinage (and other manifestations of the state) was "a stamp of Royalty," coming much too close to the habits of European monarchies and straying too far from those to be cultivated by a republican society.[38] Although none of the Treasury Department correspondence on the subject of lighthouses during this period makes any mention of such a notable feature, there is visual evidence that suggests at least the three lighthouses built by McComb included this ornament. Both Mary McComb's 1796 watercolor of Montauk Point (see Figure 6) and John McComb's 1799 elevations for the Eaton's Neck lighthouse include the head-shaped ventilator (Figure 7). Another contemporary observer, Benjamin Henry Latrobe, painted two at least watercolors of the Cape Henry lighthouse during a visit in 1798. While it is difficult to state with complete certainty that the ventilator atop the lantern is in the shape of a man's head, the most detailed of the pictures does seem to contain details that indicate the vent was more than a simple sphere (Figure 8).

It would have been completely inappropriate for American lighthouses to resemble those built by France with its absolute monarchy. The lighthouse at Cordouan, off the coast of Bordeaux, is an excellent example.[39] Its operation sustained by the collection of duties from passing ships as early as 1409, a magnificent new lighthouse was erected under royal authority beginning in 1584. It took more than twenty-five years to complete. As D. Allen Stevenson remarks, "The splendour of [Louis] de Foix's design accorded with the French tradition that buildings erected with public funds should be a credit to the period of their construction and excite the admiration of posterity," requirements that Cordouan more than met.[40] The building not only supported a lantern but also provided royal lodging should the king ever venture a visit. Had the monarch braved the treacherous currents that surrounded the islet, he would have entered the lighthouse through its "elaborate portico" adorned with Etruscan pilasters and then ascended a broad ceremonial staircase to the King's Hall. This room, occupying most of the 134 feet of the tower's diameter, had a patterned marble floor and a vaulted ceiling. The building also provided for the kingly soul, for on the third level one finds the Royal Chapel with its 11.25-meter coffered dome vault, Corinthian pilasters, and walls "richly embellished with

Figure 8. Benjamin Henry Latrobe, "View of the Lighthouse at Cape Henry, Virginia, Looking North," watercolor and ink (Baltimore: Maryland Historical Society, July 1798), 1960.108.1.4.7.

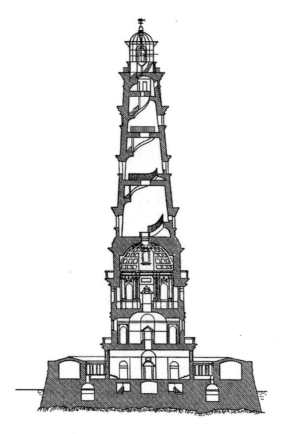

cartouches and swags."[41] Originally, this room was lit by seven dormers—a feature preserved in an early eighteenth-century renovation of the tower but removed soon after 1788, when the structure was decapitated preparatory to extending the tower and raising the lantern to a total height of 213 feet.

But this is not to suggest that the second renovation project—very nearly concurrent with the construction of the first federal lighthouses in the United States—sought to diminish the grandeur or elaborate trappings of this state building. Much to the contrary, for Joseph Teulère's design crowned the first three floors of the original tower with a dome that supported the new extension above while preserving the ornate base and ceremonial chambers below (Figure 9). Other evidence of the intention to retain the character of the building is displayed in the new tower's entablatured windows that "expressed" each of its three stages. Moreover, it is important to note that these windows are not as functional as they might seem, for the light they should provide is obscured by the spiral stairway ascending to the tower, thereby making it clear that the windows are more decorative than utilitarian. Finally, one other point provides undeniable proof that—despite the critical aid it offered to navigation and trade—the lighthouse's role had always been equally important as a manifestation of the state: from de Foix's time to the present, an inconspicuous secondary staircase has served as the mode of conveying fuel to the lantern, thereby preventing the ceremonial areas of the tower's first three levels from becoming soiled.[42] This same emphasis on the projection of state character was also a part of other eighteenth-century lighthouses in France. When the merchants of Normandy attempted to gain royal sanction and support for four lighthouses between 1765 and 1773, the government originally responded "that it did not approve of the . . . endeavor to save expense by building simple towers devoid of ornamentation, and that as such works would serve posterity they should reflect the genius of the period and accord better with the dignity of the monarch who authorized their erection."[43] Even following the French Revolution, French lighthouses retained many aspects of an ornamental form well into the nineteenth century.

Just as French lighthouses had taken on the forms of a government immersed in the traditional trappings and rituals of the authoritarian state, so too did American lighthouses become emblematic of republican modernity, utility, and restraint. Contemporary accounts placed lighthouses in the same category as other local, state, and federal government buildings. Jedidiah Morse's 1794 edition of *The American Geographer* treats a variety of public buildings, such as churches, courthouses, and lighthouses as part of a single group and on a completely equal basis. In some instances he goes even farther, giving lighthouses their own dedicated subsections within the descriptions of Massachusetts, Rhode Island, and Delaware, each of which includes a detailed description of the setting, form and dimensions of lighthouses. In describing Portland Head Light in the District of Maine and the two lighthouses in Newburyport (Massachusetts) at the mouth of the Merrimack River, Morse editorializes on the merits of investing public funds in these projects.[44] In sum, the impression is of a series of buildings that are very much an important and appropriate manifestation of the state.

By embracing best practices and utilizing the most durable materials, American lighthouses helped to promote the state's competence, credibility, and stability. The expert construction of lighthouses in stone, iron, copper, and glass incorporated the workmanship and materials necessary to stand up to the harshest conditions of their exposed locations. Although these high standards of construction guaranteed that they would fulfill their crucial navigational function, it also ensured their status as truly monumental structures that embodied far more significance than simple reckoning points.[45] The tenuous reality of federal authority also shaped lighthouses. The desires to avoid controversy when possible and to accommodate and compromise with existing constituencies when necessary were powerful forces that shaped federal policy decisions. With this in mind, those decisions most frequently favored accepted methods and models. By working cooperatively, federal authorities could progress their own strategic goal of state building through the promotion of economic unity and the projection of a recognizable state presence.

The development of a systematized network of lighthouses advanced both of these objectives. In the hands of federal officeholders, lighthouses ceased to be guides to individual harbors (and agents of local commerce) and became links between states and regions. They were instrumental in promoting coastal trade, fortifying economic bonds, and promoting the common interests of the states. In the process of doing so, lighthouses became compelling manifestations of the state. Judging them individually it was impossible to ignore their inspiring qualities: they were towering structures located in dramatic surroundings—certainly the largest manmade structure for miles around. However, to judge lighthouses of this period solely as individual structures is to miss a major aspect of their significance. Of the ten lighthouses built by the federal government between 1789 and 1799, six (Cape Henry, Ocracoke Inlet, Bald Head, Montauk Point, Highland Light on Cape Cod, and Eaton's Neck) were located in strategic locations and built in close accordance with consistent standards of design and construction.[46] Being more or less equidistant from one another and having a similar appearance, these structures presented a sense of a distributed yet unified government whose reach was extensive and whose presence was weighty. Furthermore, while their remoteness in terrestrial terms implies that they were inconspicuous, they occupied key points along busy coastal and international trade routes, where they were not only observed, but depended upon, by thousands of vessels.

Ultimately, it was the combination of individual qualities (their efficiency as instruments and their effectiveness as manifestations faithfully representing the state) and collective presence that made lighthouses objects of quiet pride rather than loud protest. These early and ambitious projects served as models for the continuous and rapid expansion of the network over the coming decades. A comparison with the British Isles highlights the magnitude of the federal program. Britain had ten lighthouses by the mid-seventeenth century, more than twenty-five by the middle of the eighteenth century, and forty-three by 1820. The United States only had thirteen in 1789, and a total of twenty-three by 1800, approximately 60 percent of the total in the British Isles. However, over the following decades lighthouse construction in the United Sates progressed at a truly amazing pace. The first dozen years of the new century saw the number of United States lighthouses nearly double to forty-five before the War of 1812 forced a temporary halt in construction (Figure 10). By 1822, the United States had seventy lighthouses, triple the number it had twenty years earlier and more than one-and-a-half times the number in the British Isles. By 1838, the United States had 204 lighthouses, an astonishing total that by 1852 had grown to 331. Furthermore, this phenomenal proliferation took place amid a climate that rejected nearly all internal improvements, thereby demonstrating their appeal across the political spectrum. The explanation can only be that lighthouses did what they were intended to do: they were successful both as instruments promoting commerce and national unity, and as appropriate manifestations of the viable, even vigorous sovereign state required to

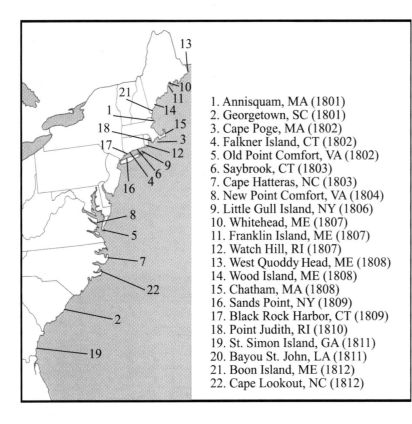

1. Annisquam, MA (1801)
2. Georgetown, SC (1801)
3. Cape Poge, MA (1802)
4. Falkner Island, CT (1802)
5. Old Point Comfort, VA (1802)
6. Saybrook, CT (1803)
7. Cape Hatteras, NC (1803)
8. New Point Comfort, VA (1804)
9. Little Gull Island, NY (1806)
10. Whitehead, ME (1807)
11. Franklin Island, ME (1807)
12. Watch Hill, RI (1807)
13. West Quoddy Head, ME (1808)
14. Wood Island, ME (1808)
15. Chatham, MA (1808)
16. Sands Point, NY (1809)
17. Black Rock Harbor, CT (1809)
18. Point Judith, RI (1810)
19. St. Simon Island, GA (1811)
20. Bayou St. John, LA (1811)
21. Boon Island, ME (1812)
22. Cape Lookout, NC (1812)

Figure 10 Lighthouses Built under Federal Authority: 1800–1812. Data from D. Alan Stevenson. *The World's Lighthouses before 1820*, 250. Map by the author.

achieve such aspirations. By mid-century, no one participating in the robust coastal trade between American ports or approaching its shores from afar could fail to perceive the presence of a strong and vital state. This was the legacy of the federal government's early forays into state building.[47]

The creation of a cohesive state requires both the development of pragmatic programs that fulfill needs not met through distributive action and the projection of a sovereign unifying authority founded on a popularly shared ideology. Lighthouses served as both instruments and manifestations of this complex endeavor throughout the formative period of the American republic.

NOTES

1. George Thatcher to Thomas B. Wait, "From a gentleman in New York to his friend," *Cumberland Gazette*, Portland, Maine, March 19, 1789; Frederick A. Muhlenberg to Benjamin Rush, March 5, 1789, both quoted in Charlene Bangs Bickford, et al., eds., *Documentary History of the First Federal Congress of the United States of America, Volume XV: March–May, 1789* (Baltimore: The Johns Hopkins University Press, 2004), 17, 37 [*DHFFC* hereafter].

2. Although the original motivation for a system of federal tonnage duties on shipping was the overall regulation of commerce on a national basis, not the support of lighthouses, the two issues were inseparable. The assumption was always that because lighthouses were funded by tonnage duties—referred to in the vernacular as "light money"—their collection fell under federal purview, and so the lighthouses themselves would too. The issue of funding for and authority over lighthouses had been anticipated and discussed as part of the debate over the commerce clause during the Constitutional Convention two years earlier. Max Farrand, *The Records of the Federal Convention of 1787*, vol. 2. (New Haven, Conn.: Yale University Press, 1966), 504, 625, 634.

3. Charlene Bangs Bickford and Helen E. Viet, eds., *DHFFC, Vol. IV: Legislative Histories, Amendments to the Constitutions through Foreign Officers Bill, 1ˢᵗ session, April–May 1789* (Baltimore: The Johns Hopkins University Press, 1986), lvii–lx.

4. S. Rufus Davis, *The Federal Principle: A Journey through Time in Search of Meaning* (Berkeley: University of California Press 1978), 114.

5. George Washington, "First Inaugural," April 20, 1789, in Theodore J. Crackel, ed. *The Papers of George Washington Digital Edition* (Charlottesville: University of Virginia Press, Rotunda, 2007), http://rotunda.upress.virginia.edu (accessed January 9, 2009).

6. Max M. Edling, *A Revolution in Favor of Government, Origins of the U.S. Constitution and the Making of the American State* (New York: Oxford University Press, 2003), 224–25.

7. Light money refers to the revenue derived from duties imposed on commerce through a particular port and earmarked for the maintenance and operation of lighthouses in that given area. The state of some lighthouses was so dire that the Boston Marine Society required members returning from sea to report "light houses not properly trimmed or attended." *Constitution and Laws of the Boston Marine Society: Instituted in the year 1742, incorporated in the year 1754* (Boston: J. Belcher, 1809), 19.

8. Ibid., 176, 178–79.

9. Charlene Bangs Bickford and Helen E. Veit, eds., *DHFFC, Vol. VI: Legislative Histories, M–U: 1st Session, April–May 1789* (Baltimore: The Johns Hopkins University Press, 1986), 1947–1959. No explicit mention of lighthouses appears in any of the six recorded versions of the Tonnage Act. Linda Grant DePauw,

Charlene Bangs Bickford, LaVonne Seigel Hauptman, eds., *DHFFC, Vol. III: Journal of the House of Representatives: 1st Session, April–May 1789* (Baltimore: The Johns Hopkins University Press, 1976), 17, 86, 103; *Historic Lighthouse Preservation Handbook* (Washington DC: National Park Service, 2001), 2–3, http://www.cr.nps.gov/maritime/handbook.html (accessed February 2, 2007).

10. "Notice is hereby given that proposals will be received . . ." *The Federal Gazette* (Philadelphia: The Federal Gazette and Philadelphia Evening Post, October 4, 1790), 3; John McComb Jr., "Memorandum & Estimates, Receipts," 1798, Papers of John McComb Jr. (New York: New-York Historical Society), 4; John McComb, "Memorandum Book, BV," Papers of John McComb (New York: New-York Historical Society), 5. In various places McComb ambiguously indicates the cost of the Sandy Hook lighthouse as both £5,669 and £5,341. The construction and maintenance of Sandy Hook also bears the characteristics of the well-established process carried on between citizens, interest groups (particularly the Chamber of Commerce of the City of New York), and government (here New York and New Jersey). As was nearly always the case, "light money" was raised through the imposition of duties on tonnage passing through the port. "Architectural History of the Lighthouse," typescript (Montauk, N.Y.: Montauk Historical Society), 16. Abisha Woodward built three Connecticut lighthouses under federal authority between 1800 and 1803, all of which followed the Sandy Hook prototype. A circular plan for a lighthouse was nearly unheard of south of Cape Cod during this period. However, north of the Cape, with Boston Light's circular form predating this period, some but not all lighthouses continued to follow that familiar form.

11. D. Alan Stevenson, *The World's Lighthouses before 1920* (London: Oxford University Press, 1959), 178. Regarding the issue of "superfluities" generally, see Drew R. McCoy, "Republicanism and American Foreign Policy: James Madison and the Political Economy of Commercial Discrimination, 1789 to 1794," *The William and Mary Quarterly*, 3rd ser., vol. 31, no. 4. (October 1974), 642, http://links.jstor.org/sici?sici=0043-5597%281974l0%293%3A31%3A4%3C633%3ARAAFPJ%3E2.0.CO%3B2-D (accessed February 12, 2007).

12. Bangs Bickford and Veit, eds., *DHFFC*, vol. V, 1248–1254; *A petition of the tradesmen, manufacturers,*

and others of the town of Baltimore, in the State of Maryland . . . praying for an imposition of such duties on all foreign articles, April 11, 1789, quoted in Grant DePauw, Bangs Bickford, Seigel Hauptman, eds., *DHFFC*, vol. III, 17; Harold C. Syrett, ed., *The Papers of Alexander Hamilton*, vol. 5 (New York: Columbia University Press, 1962), Jacob Wray to Alexander Hamilton, October 12, 1789, 424.

13. Thomas Randell and William Heyer to Alexander Hamilton, December 1, 1789, Letters Received by the Treasury Department, National Archives Record Group 26, 1785–1812, Volume 5, Connecticut and New York, 1789–1805; Syrett ed., *Papers of Alexander Hamilton*, vol. 5, Joseph Otis to A. Hamilton, November 11, 1789, 512; Mungo MacKay to A. Hamilton, November 16, 1789, 517; Tobias Lear to A. Hamilton, November 21, 1789, 534.

14. Compensation for the keepers was yet to be determined, but Collectors of Customs were to receive supplementary compensation equivalent to a percentage of the tonnage duty they collected. Interestingly, this form of compensation continued into the 1850s without formal Congressional authorization.

15. Syrett, ed., *Papers of Alexander Hamilton*, vol. 6, A. Hamilton to George Washington, January 3, 1790, 42. Hamilton did not include information on lighthouses in Rhode Island because that state had not yet ratified the Constitution.

16. Syrett, ed., *Papers of Alexander Hamilton*, vol. 6, Request for Supplemental Appropriation, March 1, 1790, 281; Contractual Parameters, A. Hamilton to Benjamin Lincoln, March 10, 1790, 297; William Allibone to A. Hamilton, August 1, 1790, 514; Report on Additional Sums Necessary for the Support of the Government, August 5, 1790, 520–42; Benjamin Lincoln to A. Hamilton, August 17, 1790, 560; William Allibone to A. Hamilton, August 20, 1790, 561; William Allibone to A. Hamilton, August 21, 1790, 561; Tobias Lear to A. Hamilton, August 24, 1790, 565; A. Hamilton to William Allibone, August 25, 1790(?), 565.

17. Syrett, ed., *Papers of Alexander Hamilton*, vol. 6, A. Hamilton to Thomas Newton Jr. June 19, 1790, 468; Th. Newton Jr., to A. Hamilton, June 27, 1790, 474; Th. Newton Jr., to A. Hamilton, July 11, 1790, 491; Th. Newton Jr., to A. Hamilton, August 6, 1790, 546; Th. Newton Jr., to A. Hamilton, August 7, 1790, 549.

18. Syrett, ed., *Papers of Alexander Hamilton*, vol. 7, A. Hamilton to G. Washington, January 5, 1791, 412–15; McComb, "Memorandum Book, BV," *Papers of John*

McComb (New York Historical Society), 7; Harold C. Syrett, ed., *Papers of Alexander Hamilton*, vol. 8 (New York: Columbia University Press, 1965), A. Hamilton to Richard Harrison, April 1, 1791, 236, fn 2; Ron Chernow, *Alexander Hamilton* (New York: Penguin Press, 2004), 30–32. One final factor almost certainly played a part in Hamilton's decision. As a fellow New Yorker he was close to those who recommended McComb, including Chief Justice John Jay. McComb also "produced a letter from Messrs. Nicholas Cruger and Peter Kremble of New York as his sureties," effectively securing the government's financial risk. The significance of this is that as a youth, Hamilton had been the protégé of the Cruger family in whose business he had worked and who had been instrumental in his move from the Caribbean to New York. It is also worth noting that although this was the first documented encounter between Hamilton and McComb, it was far from their last. In addition to his other work for the federal government, McComb designed and built Hamilton's Northern Manhattan country home, Hamilton Grange, completed in 1802.

19. Syrett, ed., *Papers of Alexander Hamilton*, vol. 7, Tobias Lear to A. Hamilton, January 11, 1791, 425.

20. Th. Newton Jr., ca. 1881, quoted in Kraig Anderson, "Old Cape Henry, VA," *Lighthouse Friends.com*, http://www.lighthousefriends.com/light.asp?ID=448 (accessed February 17, 2007). Not of less import—at least to McComb—were the associated negotiations about the additional cost of the work (eventually agreed as $2,500).

21. "Architectural History of the Lighthouse," 12; *Annals of Congress: The Debate and Proceedings in the Congress of the United States, Second Congress, October 24, 1791–March 2, 1793* (Washington D.C.: Gales & Seaton, 1849), 97, 101, 110, 1356.

22. William Randell to T. Coxe, December 26, 1792, Joseph Anthony to T. Coxe, January 8, 1793, Letters Received by the Treasury Department, National Archives Record Group 26, 1785–1812, vol. 5, Connecticut and New York, 1789–1805.

23. *An Act of Cession*, by New York State, December 26, 1792, Lighthouse Site Files, National Archives Record Group 26, Records of the U.S. Coast Guard, 1785–1992, Box 136: New York no. 64, Long Beach Bar, to New York no. 76 Fort Niagara; Henry P. Dering to Coxe, August 31, 1795, Letters Received by the Treasury Department, National Archives Record Group 26, 1785–1812, vol. 5, Connecticut and New York,

1789–1805; "Return of the Whole Number of Persons in the Several Districts of the United States," 1790 (Philadelphia: 1793), United States Census Bureau, online:*http://www2.census.gov/prod2/decennial/documents/1790a-01.pdf* (accessed March 22, 2008).

24. Syrett ed., *Papers of Alexander Hamilton*, vol. 13, T. Coxe to A. Hamilton, January 3, 1793, 447; Adam Grace, "Federal-State Negotiations over Federal Enclaves in the Early Republic" (The Berkeley Electronic Press, Paper No. 509, 2005), 17–18, http://law.bepress.com/cgi/viewcontent.cgi?article=2585&context=expresso (accessed January 6, 2007).

25. Randolph wrote, "when I adverted to the act . . . it became obvious, that congress did not mean to accept this cession, with a mutilated jurisdiction," one that essentially provided for concurrent federal and state jurisdiction rather than a sole federal one. "It is manifest," Randolph added, "that this has not been done, and therefore the act of New York is not commensurate with the Act of Congress." Edmond Randolph to A. Hamilton, January 7, 1793, Letters Received by the Treasury Department, vol. 5, National Archives RG-26.

26. In the fall of 1793, Coxe wrote to the New York State Congressional delegation to inform them, "It appears . . . that due consideration of the subject may produce about the beginning of the next session a suggestion from the executive in favor of a new act of Congress . . . proceeding on the Idea of a concurrent jurisdiction." The following January, Washington did exactly that, sending a message to Congress asking that they revisit the original legislation. Grace, "Federal-State Negotiations over Federal Enclaves in the Early Republic," 17–18.

27. Joseph Anthony to T. Coxe, January 8, 1793, C. Miller to Thomas Randell, January 14, 1793, Patrick Dennis to T. Coxe, December 9, 1793, Letters Received by the Treasury Department, vol. 5, National Archives RG-26.

28. The sellers of the site on Turtle Hill demanded that usage of the land be restricted to lighthouses and their associated structures. Although this restriction was included in the original Virginia cession, here it was being requested not by a state but by a private party. Nevertheless, perhaps because the government had no other intention and was eager to get construction underway, this concession was granted and included in the registered deed of sale. The sellers also requested that they retain the "authority right and power to remove and dislodge any fisherman or

other persons who might come [to the property] to reside and who were trespassers." This demand was fiercely promoted by the sellers, but ultimately it was rejected because it implied the federal government's sanction of extralegal vigilante action. Perhaps as a conciliatory gesture, the government agreed to pay for the construction and maintenance of "any partition or fence" bordering the property. Henry P. Dering to T. Coxe, August 31, 1795, Letters Received by the Treasury Department, vol. 5, National Archives RG-26; Recorded Deed for Turtle Hill, Montauk, New York, January 16, 1796, Lighthouse Site Files, National Archives Record Group 26, Box 136.

29. McComb, "Memorandum & Estimates, Receipts, John McComb, Jr., 1798," 14; "Architectural History of the Lighthouse," 13.

30. This may well account for the willingness of Congress to continue to invest in them in contrast to other internal improvement projects.

31. H. Dering to T. Coxe, April 23, 1796, H. Dering to T. Coxe, June 1, 1796, H. Dering to T. Coxe, June 20, 1796, H. Dering to T. Coxe, October 10, 1796, H. Dering to T. Coxe, November 18, 1796, all in Letters Received by the Treasury Department, vol. 5, National Archives RG-26. McComb's suggestion to locate the lighthouse farther back than the specified 130 yards from the bluffs was well-founded. Soon after construction was completed on the tower and other buildings, it was necessary to build three dams closing off gullies that threatened to accelerate the erosion of the soft cliffs that wrapped around three sides of Turtle Hill. This problem plagues the site even today, with the battle to retard the cliffs' retreat assuming ever increasing urgency. The distance between the edge of the bluffs and the lighthouse is barely more than one-tenth of the original distance. John McComb, "Plan of the Buildings on Montauk Point," drawing, 1796, Lighthouse Plans and Maps, National Archives (College Park, Md.) Record Group 26, Montauk Point, New York no. 2; Cornelia Dean, "The Coastline Is Retreating. Should the Montauk Lighthouse Stand Its Ground," *New York Times*, November 21, 2006, http://select.nytimes.com/search/restricted/article?res=F70611F63E5A0C728EDDA80994 (accessed April 11, 2007).

32. H. Dering to T. Coxe, December 18, 1796, H. Dering to T. Coxe, January 16, 1797, both in Letters Received by the Treasury Department, vol. 5, National Archives RG-26.

33. Timothy Dwight, *Travels in New England and New York*, 4 vols., edited by Barbara Miller Solomon (Cambridge, Mass.: Belkamp Press, Harvard University Press, 1969), 3:218.

34. This system of spatial reference was echoed in other circumstances. For example, in his widely read *The American Geography*, Jedidiah Morse specifies the latitude for Boston Harbor, Cape Ann, Cape Cod, Narragansett Bay, Montauk Point, Cape Henlopen, and Cape Henry but never indicates their longitude. Jedidiah Morse, *The American Geography; or a View of the Present Situation of the United States of America* (London: John Stockdale, Piccadilly, 1794).

35. Joshua C. Taylor, *America as Art* (Washington, D.C.: The Smithsonian Institute, 1976), 3, 15–16; John Norman, *The American Pilot; Containing the Navigation of the Sea Coast of North America* (Boston: John Norman, 1791); Edmund Blunt, *The American Coast Pilot* (Newburyport, Mass.: Blunt, 1796).

36. "Notice . . ." *The Federal Gazette*, October 4, 1790, 3; "The First Contract for the Construction of a Lighthouse for the Federal Government." *Lighthouse Service Bulletin* 5, no. 37 (Washington DC: US Coast Guard, January, 1939), 151–52. As referred to elsewhere in this article, the only substantial deviation between the contract and the finished building was the depth and breadth of the foundation, the alterations to which are also detailed in this source.

37. The "First Contract" also specified the dimensions and materials for two other buildings: "a frame House twenty feet square and two stories high, with a frame kitchen for the occupation & residence of the keeper of the Light House, and . . . finish the same with Lath and plaister [sic]"; and "build and finish in stone . . . a Vault, twelve feet wide and twenty feet in length, for the storage & safekeeping of the Oil . . . which vault shall be arched and covered over with Sand or Earth . . . and furnish the said vault with eight strong Cedar Cisterns with Covers, each capable of containing two hundred gallons of Oil."

38. *Annals of Congress*, 484.

39. Stevenson, *World's Lighthouses*, 21, 30, 60.

40. Ibid., 31.

41. Douglas B. Hague and Rosemary Christie, *Lighthouses: Their Architecture, History, and Archaeology* (Llanddysul, Wales: Gomer Press, 1975), 19–20, 119–20; Stevenson, *World's Lighthouses*, 197.

42. Hague and Christie, *Lighthouses*, 119.

43. Stevenson, *World's Lighthouses*, 189.

44. Morse, *American Geography*, 314, 319, 344, 453. In writing about North Carolina (which was as yet without a lighthouse), Morse noted the dangers of navigating the Outer Banks and the resulting impediment to the trade and commerce of the state; 518.

45. Nora Pat Small, "The Lighthouse on the Eastern Seaboard, 1789–1900," unpublished typescript (Charlottesville: School of Architecture, University of Virginia, 1981), 6.

46. Of the four that do not fit neatly within this paradigm, the state began Portland Head prior to the imposition of federal authority; two other lighthouses in Maine (Seguin Island and Baker's Island) were located near harbor entrances but also on prominent landmarks between New England the Canadian maritime provinces, and one, Gay Head, marks Martha Vineyard in the heavily traveled waters leading to the eastern entrance to Long Island Sound and the Connecticut coastal region. All except Gay Head (which was built of wood) utilized the construction materials and techniques outlined above.

47. Stevenson, *World's Lighthouses*, 250; Dennis L. Noble, *Lighthouses and Keepers: The U.S. Lighthouse Service and Its Legacy* (Annapolis: Naval Institute Press, 1997), 12.

TRAVIS E. NYGARD AND PAMELA H. SIMPSON

Indians at the Corn Palaces

Race and Reception at Two Midwestern Festival Buildings

In the late nineteenth century, fall harvest festivals took a peculiarly spectacular form in a number of Midwestern cities. Huge grain palaces, constructed of wood but covered inside and out with mosaics made from ears of corn and various colored grasses, became the centerpieces for the celebrations.[1] Sioux City, Iowa, built five corn palaces between 1887 and 1891 (Figure 1). When floods prevented Sioux City from carrying out plans for another in 1892, Mitchell, South Dakota, took on the idea and, with a few interruptions, has had a corn palace ever since (Figure 2). Cities in Iowa, Kansas, Missouri, and Texas had their own versions as well. The extraordinary effort expended to erect these buildings required the cooperation of an entire community. In Sioux City, for example, they were used for less than a month and then reconstructed or reclad the next year. Because they reflected the agendas of numerous constituencies, the palaces allow the modern scholar to explore how identities shaped the buildings and also how the buildings helped to shape those identities. This is particularly true in terms of race. A close look at the Sioux City and Mitchell corn palaces clearly demonstrates that these are places where Native Americans and Euro-Americans came together to negotiate their places in society. Two time periods offer an informative contrast. The first was the late nineteenth century, when the phenomenon was new and, although instigated by white people, involved Native Americans as subjects and participants. The second was in the mid-twentieth century, when the Mitchell Corn Palace was reinterpreted by a Native American artist.

Figure 1. The 1887 Sioux City, Iowa, Corn Palace, from *Frank Leslie's Weekly*, October 8, 1887, 125. Authors' collection.

Figure 2. Mitchell, South Dakota, 1892 Corn Palace under construction. Courtesy of Mitchell Area Historical Society.

Understanding buildings in terms of identity is a tall order. After all, "identity" is a multifaceted concept, the very thing that makes it powerful. Historians Rogers Brubaker and Frederick Cooper recently analyzed how scholars use the term, noting its paradoxical aspects. Identity can refer to self-labeling, self-understanding, membership in a group, feelings of belonging, categorization by others, empathetic connections with others, motivations for social change, sameness with or difference from others, a core essence, something deeply ingrained, or something superficial. Furthermore, identities can be either static or fluid.[2] How, then, does identity relate to the corn palaces? To answer this question, we will focus on a symbolic reading of the iconography of the buildings, especially as it appeared in its decorative panels, as well as on the performative events that took place there. As is typical of community-based construction, the corn palaces were contested spaces. Both Indians and white people, with varying degrees of agreement, informed the meanings that these buildings held. How they should be constructed, what imagery should adorn them, and whose values should be celebrated are key issues with which the communities wrestled when first erecting the buildings, and they continue to be debated today.

Spatially, the corn palaces were simple. They were fundamentally festival centers designed for maximum flexibility. The interiors were large open spaces that usually centered on a concert hall and stage with side aisles, balconies, and a second floor for exhibition areas. The present-day Mitchell Corn Palace is similar; it serves as a municipal auditorium, a basketball arena, and a stage to host high school proms, conventions, and sporting events. The buildings were also decidedly urban, usually located in the heart of the commercial center of the town; the purpose of the corn festivals was to draw visitors, investors, and new settlers to the community. The architectural form, as is readily apparent in the historic photographs of the corn palaces, was a festive, exotic eclecticism, with towers, domes, and turrets that borrowed from architectural traditions across the globe.

What was new, however, was the decoration, and especially the materials used to create it. The

structures were covered with murals made from real ears of corn, either split lengthwise or cut crosswise. Artisans nailed different-colored ears to the wooden surface to form decorative patterns. Bundles of grasses or sorghum held together with wire created borders and covered surfaces. Some areas contained geometric designs; others featured panels with representational imagery. In a region where sod walls and thatched roofs were common in the late nineteenth century, the cladding and roofing of the corn palaces in vegetative materials may have seemed consistent with local building traditions. But the purpose of corn-palace cladding was decorative and symbolic; corn was not only the main decorative feature—it was what the palaces were intended to celebrate. It is in this context that Indians appeared frequently as a decorative theme.

The connections between corn and Indians are, to some extent, obvious. Corn is a New World product. Within the upper Midwest, the Yanktonai band of the Nakota people[3]—a member of which, Oscar Howe, would design mosaics for the Mitchell Corn Palace in the mid-twentieth century—raised at least three varieties of corn during the nineteenth century.[4] The German explorer Prince Maximilian of Wied described the colors grown by the Mandan in the area in 1833 as "White, Yellow, Red, Spotted Black and sweet maize; very hard yellow maize, white or red striped maize, and very tender yellow maize."[5] Corn appears in the visual imagery of many New World cultures, and it was one of the symbols Latrobe used in trying to create an American iconography for the U.S. Capitol.[6] In the late nineteenth century, the symbolic meaning of corn received national attention when in 1893 Candace Wheeler, the well-known New York textile artist, led a lobbying effort to have Congress declare corn the national floral emblem. "From time immemorial," she wrote, "the primitive peoples of this Western world . . . paid homage to it in rituals and songs and dances." No other plant "is so typical of our greatness and prosperity," no other plant so "historically American."[7]

Corn also featured prominently in one of the most popular pieces of literature of the period—Longfellow's epic poem *The Song of Hiawatha*.[8] Using an origin myth drawn largely from the Ojibwe—a people who historically lived to the northeast of Sioux City in present-day Minnesota and Wisconsin—Longfellow told a tale of a beautiful corn god named Mondamin, who appeared to Hiawatha and informed him that they would wrestle for three days. On the third day, when Hiawatha defeated him, he was to bury the god and water the grave. Hiawatha did so and the corn plant sprang forth. The ripened corn became the gift that would feed Hiawatha's people (Figure 3).[9] Corn Palace officials often retold this story during the opening ceremonies, local papers reprinted parts of the poem, and decorators included images of Hiawatha and Mondamin in their panels.[10] The legend about the origin of corn held such meaning for Sioux City residents that local women hosted "Mondamin luncheons" at which every course was a form of corn (e.g., corn soup, corn fritters, corn-fed beef, corn pudding), the luncheon space was decorated with corn stalks and husks, and the entertainment included songs about corn and a recitation of the Hiawatha poem. A Sioux City men's group named the Mondamin Club organized supporters of the Corn Palace.[11]

Although Hiawatha and Mondamin were two of the most frequently seen Indian images at the corn palaces, there were many other examples of Indian imagery made from grain. For example, the Santa Fe Railroad—sponsor and promoter of many Kansas corn festivals in the 1890s and early 1900s—used the Indian as its official logo and created a gigantic street sculpture of a corn-covered Indian for display (Figure 4). Much of this phenomenon seems to have been motivated by the interests of white people, and it can be understood as part of a wider phenomenon observed by scholars. Indeed, historians have examined how white people "played" as Indians, fantasized about "going Native," and commercialized indigenous culture. Such activities often reinforced the stereotypes of the era and positioned white people as dominant during a time of profound cultural change.[12]

The question of why Indian peoples took part in the festivities surrounding grain palaces, however, is more difficult to answer. Such participation was not an isolated phenomenon. In 1902, at the Atchison, Kansas, Festival, a mandolin

Figure 3. *Dead He Lay There in the Sunset*, M. L. Kirk illustration of the death of Mondamin and the birth of corn for Longfellow's *The Story of Hiawatha* (New York: Frederick A. Stokes Co, 1910), 22. Author's collection.

Figure 5. Indians at 1913 Mitchell, South Dakota Corn Palace. Courtesy of Mitchell Area Historical Society.

orchestra made up of sixteen students from the Chilocco, Oklahoma, Indian school entertained onlookers from a platform beneath the giant statue.[13] In Sioux City in 1887, Indians from the nearby Winnebago Reservation not only marched and rode in opening parades, but some of the women participated in "Squaw Races."[14] Indians even contributed a booth to the interior, where they showed their own homegrown corn and vegetables.[15] At Mitchell's first corn palace festival in 1892, an Indian brass band from the Santee Reservation performed in concert, and other Indians paraded in war bonnets and face paint while giving war whoops to delight the crowd (Figure 5).[16] One of the entertainments that year was to be an Indian wedding, but when the bride and groom didn't show up, Indian musicians from the band filled in as substitutes with comic cross-dressing, exaggerated costumes, and axle grease as facial decoration.[17]

Tamed, subdued, and no longer a threat, Indians could be a form of entertainment to their white audiences, and they could even be invited to participate in the festivities, although the participation came in two limited forms. Either the Indians were invited to "play" Indian by showing traditional costumes, giving war whoops, or demonstrating physical prowess in foot races, or they were invited to demonstrate their newly

found "civilized skills" with band music and agricultural displays. In both cases, the performance reinforced white values, policies, and views of history. In 1887, a Sioux City reporter provided a chilling assessment of what the corn palaces meant to white–Indian relations when he wrote that white settlers in the 1850s had formed a "vanguard of the mighty army which drove out the red man and made his hunting ground a corn-field, the greatest and richest in the world. And then to make the thing more binding they have at last set up a Palace to the corn king at Sioux City to which, as if in fate's deep sarcasm, they have invited back the Indians as guests."[18] Such a historical shift was indeed occurring, driven by national policy. In 1887—the same year the first corn palace was built—the U.S. Congress passed the Dawes Act. This legislation abolished the communal holding of land on reservations in favor of small, individually held parcels. The ostensive goal was for Indians to abandon long-standing strategies of communal subsistence and become Jeffersonian family farmers. The policy was to make the Indians "civilized" by making them adopt white practices.[19] Their old ways were "savage," whereas the new ones, especially those demonstrated in the music and agricultural displays, were evidence of the success of white policies. Although the Sioux City reporter's remarks may have had an

Figure 6. Gregory, South Dakota, Registration Office, 1911, decorated with corn murals. Courtesy of Mitchell Area Historical Society.

overtone of irony, he left no doubt that the white settlers had triumphed, and that the Corn Palace was a symbol of that conquest.

Another example of white conquest came in 1910, when the Registration Office at Gregory, South Dakota, was decorated with corn murals (Figure 6). Although the Dawes Act and four subsequent acts seem on the surface to have been attempts to give Indians private ownership of land, one key provision was that after the allotments were made, the "left-over" land could be sold to white settlers. In 1910–1911, the Rose Bud and Pine Ridge Reservation lands in Bennett and Mellette counties were opened, and homesteaders could apply for them at certain designated registration points.[20] One of those was in Gregory. The building housing the office was a one-story structure with a central ogee dome and two side entrances. Located on Main Street, it was covered with corn murals depicting an Indian in a war bonnet, a horned steer, a central U.S. shield, and abstract Indian motifs. Floyd Gillis, the main decorator for the Mitchell Corn Palace, executed the murals, and in fact they are nearly identical to features that he made for the 1910 Corn Palace. The irony of using Indian imagery to ornament a building dedicated to selling Indian lands to white settlers makes it clear that corn art was used in the service of white triumph.

In light of white views such as those just described, we might ask why the Indians took part in the corn palace festivities at all, and what their participation might have meant to them, as opposed to what it meant to the white audience. Evidence is scant, because the Indians wrote little about the festivals; accounts that do exist are often filtered through a white retelling. Still, they do give us some material for interpretation. One most obvious conclusion is that at a time when official governmental policy was a heavy-handed attempt to "civilize" natives by wiping out their cultures, when it was common to take children away from the reservation to put them in Indian schools where they were forbidden to use their language; when the Indian Bureau forbade the performance of Indian rituals such as dances,[21] these grain-covered buildings filled with exhibition booths and celebrated with parades, concerts, and sporting events at least acknowledged an Indian presence and gave Indians some avenue for expression of their traditions.

The aforementioned desire on the part of Indians to find new venues for asserting their values might account for the widespread participation described in the press. For example, the newspaper account of the opening parade for the 1887 Sioux City Corn Palace reported that nearly 200 Indians from the Omaha, Sioux, and Winnebago tribes participated. "About seventy five of the adult Indians were mounted. They were in full war paint and decked out with feathers, skins of wild animals, bright-colored prints and gaudy cloths and with faces smeared with vermilion." Behind them came "wagons . . . full of younger Indians, squaws and papooses . . . in gala day attire." The writer commented, "It may be doubted whether any of the throngs of people better enjoyed the entertainment than those Indians who were so prominent a feature of it. The men and women . . . chatted jollily as they rode along. And the . . . children gazed with wide-open mouths at the decorations." One warrior on horseback, "put everyone under lasting obligation by ever and anon giving forth the genuine, old-fashioned aboriginal war-whoop . . . and they cheered him for it heartily."[22] If we can read beyond the condescending tone of the reporter, and think about the experience of the Indians rather than the white crowd, it seems that the parading Indians were acting on their own agency and enjoyed performing.

As with the Wild West shows, the Indian themes presented at the palaces and the Indians' participation in parades may have contributed to a misleading stereotype, but at the same time they affirmed certain aspects of Indian identity. As one performer in Buffalo Bill's show explained, "We were raised on horseback; that is the way we had to work. These men furnished us the same work we were raised to; that is the reason we want to work."[23] In other words, they had logical reasons to participate in the Wild West shows (for pay and also for the chance to demonstrate their horsemanship). By extension, we could assert that even without renumeration, they chose to participate in the festival parades for the chance to show off their skills. This point also applies to their contribution of their own corn and vegetables to exhibitions at grain palaces. While national policy attempted to encourage farming among Native people, and newspaper accounts of the time claimed the displays as evidence of that success, among the Dakota and tribes in eastern South Dakota and northern Iowa and Nebraska there already were farming traditions. Rather than seeing the Indian display of agricultural products as signs of a newly won civilization imposed by the white conquerors, the Indians

might have intended the displays as expressions of their long-held agricultural practices and as evidence that their skills were equal to those of whites. There is even some evidence that, with the encouragement of the Indian Bureau, some Indians appropriated the agricultural fair as a form they could use to their own advantage.[24] On the Crow Creek Reservation, for example, from 1906 to 1911, there were annual fairs with agricultural displays, grain art, demonstrations of Indian crafts, and even Indian dances—the bureau disapproved of the latter, but the Indians used the fairs as an excuse to demonstrate their traditions.[25]

The story of Indians at the corn palaces may start with white appropriation of Indian themes, but it also incorporates Indian participation for their own purposes, and even Indian use of palaces and agricultural fairs to help shape their own identities. The most compelling example of the latter, however, comes in the second part of our story, the developments at the Mitchell, South Dakota, Corn Palace.

Sioux City had, as it proudly proclaimed, invented the grain palace form, and most Midwesterners expected it to continue the tradition. It was a shock not only to Sioux City folk but to everyone in the region when devastating floods in the spring of 1892 caused the city fathers to abandon their plans for the Corn Palace that year.

Louis Beckwith and Lawrence Gale, from Mitchell, South Dakota, saw the crisis in Sioux City as an opportunity and decided their town should have its own corn palace. They canvassed the community and raised $3,700 for the project. They also traveled to Sioux City to talk to organizers and received not only help and advice, but also the promise that C. P. Brown—the architect for the whole series of Sioux City palaces—would design theirs, and that Col. Alexander Rohe, the Kansan who had decorated the last Sioux City palace, would similarly adorn theirs.[26] A Mitchell businessman donated a vacant lot on Main Street. A local builder constructed a 66 x 100 foot building, and seemingly every man, woman, and child in Mitchell was involved in the effort to decorate it. Local farmers contributed grains and grasses. Local ladies decorated the interior. Even children showed up for duties in preparing the grains for

Figure 7. Mitchell,
South Dakota, 1903
Corn Palace. Courtesy of
Mitchell Area Historical
Society.

the decorators. In an amazing fifty-nine days, the people of Mitchell completed their first corn palace. A huge effort was made in advertising, and special excursion cars were booked with the railroads. "If grit and hustle are sufficient to make a success," declared the *Sioux Falls Press*, "then the Corn Belt Exposition to be held in Mitchell will be all that its most ardent friends could desire."[27]

It was such a success that no one doubted the tradition had to continue. There was another, even larger corn palace built in 1893. But, like many places, in 1894 Mitchell ran into trouble. The national financial panic caught up with the city, and then there was a severe drought. The people thus did not use their corn palace for six years, but in 1900 the tradition was revived, and Lawrence Gale once again led the effort. That year William Jennings Bryan lent his eloquent oratory to the event. The tradition was reestablished and, with only a few exceptions, Mitchell has had a corn palace ever since. Unlike Sioux City, which tore down and rebuilt a wooden structure every

year, Mitchell reused the same wooden core for each of its palaces from 1893 to 1904—a building left unadorned during the dry years of 1892 to 1904 (Figure 7). One of the most elaborate efforts was in 1904, when Mitchell was bidding to become the capital of the state. The town persuaded John Philip Sousa to bring his band to the festival, and the crowds and publicity were bigger than ever. In 1905 Mitchell decided to build a still larger palace, 125 x 142 feet, and to move it to a new lot about a block away from the original site. In 1919, concerned about safety, they decided to build yet another, of fireproof materials that could be used year-round. With a $100,000 bond issue, the town commissioned Cornelius W. and George Rapp of Chicago, esteemed movie theater designers, to build this last one (Figure 8). Made of concrete and steel, with designated sections for crop mosaics, it was finished in 1921. It is the core of the building that still stands in 2010, an active institution to this day.[28] Both the form and decoration of this last building were rethought

Figure 8. Cornelius and George Rapp's permanent Corn Palace, Mitchell, South Dakota, completed 1921. Courtesy of Mitchell Area Historical Society.

several times, most notably for our discussion in 1948, when the Corn Palace Committee hired a Native American painter, Oscar Howe, to redesign it.[29]

Although documentation from the committee does not survive, in retrospect the group seems to have been open to the idea of presenting the history of the region in a new manner. Rather than reiterating a one-dimensional narrative of white settlement and conquest, as the first corn palaces had, they chose someone who would represent a Native American point of view.

Oscar Howe (Figure 9) was born in 1915 on the Crow Creek Indian Reservation, in the eastern part of South Dakota.[30] As was typical of the time, government policy forced him, at age seven, to leave his family to go to the Indian School in Pierre, where he experienced the worst

of assimilation policy. Denied his language and culture, and beaten for any infraction or lapse, he had a reprieve at age ten when school officials sent him home for a year due to health problems. He later claimed this year was one of the most important in his life. His grandmother took care of him and used that time to teach him about his culture and to share with him traditional stories and images. He was a talented artist, a fact later recognized when he was chosen to be one of the few sent to Santa Fe in 1935 to study art under Dorothy Dunn. Working with the Smithsonian as part of a New Deal program, Dunn had the idea of letting Native artists study historical Native art to use it as the basis for developing a distinctive Native American modern art practice. The result was the "Studio Style," with flattened forms, clear outlines, little modeling, and muted earth-toned colors. Artists associated with Dunn often celebrated themes referring back to historical traditions, as can be seen in an example by Howe, the painting *Deer Hunt* from 1947 (Figure 10).[31]

Howe had some early successes with the style and executed several WPA-sponsored murals, including one for the Mitchell Carnegie Library's dome.[32] He was drafted into the army in 1942, served in Europe, and met his future wife in Germany. When he returned after the war, he settled in Mitchell and worked out an arrangement with the local college, Dakota Wesleyan, to both attend as an undergraduate and be a paid artist in residence, with some teaching duties. Thus he was a local artist with some fame in 1948, when the Corn Palace Committee asked him to take on the duties of designing the annual murals. He did so, from 1948 to 1971.

From the very first, Howe made it clear that his mosaics would reflect not only his own "modern Indian art" style, but also an Indian iconography. In a 1948 newspaper interview, he explained:

> This decorative designing of the panels on the Corn Palace is my first attempt to do modern Indian art with the unique media of corn and grain. . . . I am very much interested in it and so have tried to carry out my ideas of Indian symbolism and the modern flat Indian art works. . . . The use of corn and grain in decoration is unique and most fitting. I feel greatly honored in designing the Corn Palace.[33]

His work at the palace, spanning twenty-four years, was concurrent with his rethinking of Native American art traditions. Among art historians, Howe is best known for abandoning the Studio Style and passionately bolstering the use of abstraction among Native artists.

Howe's enthusiasm clashed with norms upheld by conservatives in the Indian art community, and in 1958 his work was subsequently rejected from the prestigious Philbrook Museum of Art's Indian Annual exhibition for not being "traditional Indian painting." His biting protest, expressed in a letter to the curator, asked, "Are we to be held back forever with one phase of Indian painting, with no right for individualism, dictated to as the Indian has always been, put on

reservations and treated like a child, and only the White Man knows what is best for him? . . . Well, I am not going to stand for it." His closing hope in this letter was that "the Art World will not be one more contributor to holding us in chains." Such words and artwork were highly effective, and they ultimately led to an acceptance and celebration of new forms of representation among his peers.[34]

As Howe and several of his biographers have noted, his work with grain mosaic patterns on the Mitchell Corn Palace influenced this shift in his painting style.[35] Indeed, working with ears of

Figure 9. Oscar Howe standing in front of the Corn Palace, Mitchell, South Dakota. Courtesy of University of South Dakota.

Figure 10. Oscar Howe's *Deer Hunt*, 1947, casein on paper. Courtesy of U.S. Department of the Interior, Indian Arts and Crafts Board, Washington D.C.

Figure 11. Oscar Howe's designs for the 1948 Mitchell, South Dakota, Corn Palace (postcard, author's collection). Art reproduced courtesy of Mitchell Corn Palace and City of Mitchell.

corn by necessity involves reducing imagery to key geometric features, a characteristic evident in his earliest murals. Howe's first theme in 1948 was to be, appropriately enough, the Origin of Corn, and he chose not the Ojibwa legend from *Hiawatha,* but one from his own Yanktonai Dakota tradition. The theme was significant enough to Howe that he executed two paintings based on it and later, in 1962, would do another panel of it for the inside of the Corn Palace.

Directly above the entrance to the Corn Palace, Howe installed his version (Figure 11). Composed with bilateral symmetry, the cycle's central panel showed a single cornstalk rising from the earth, bordered by stepped rectangles that Howe identified as tepees. Centrally placed above the growing corn plant was the nurturing bison sun (a circle with horns), an important Dakota symbol. Two panels on either side of the central one presented ceremonial Indian maidens holding ears of corn in each hand. Because the iconography related to the origin of corn might not have been immediately recognizable by most non-Native viewers, Howe explained the symbolism in the local newspaper and then expanded upon it a year later, when he made a painting of the same theme for Nebraska City. The legend was that the Dakota people encountered a female bison whose swollen udder dripped milk onto the earth. Overnight, the drops formed a column and then grew into the first corn plant. Deemed a

gift from the Great Spirit, it was cultivated by the Dakota people.[36]

Howe flanked the central panels with two other, larger mosaics that seemed to offer opposing historical traditions (Figure 12). On the right, an Indian on horseback rode along the crest of a hill and aimed a bow and arrow at three bison. All the figures were in silhouette against a background that suggested a rough terrain—likely the Badlands. Buffalo hunting was the means of survival for many nomadic Midwestern Indian tribes before Europeans arrived, and doing so from horseback became the norm after that animal's introduction from about 1750 to 1850.[37] A complementary panel on the left side of the façade depicted ranching. Organized as a mirror image of the other scene, the ranching panel repeated the positions of a rider and three animals silhouetted against an identical landscape. This time, however, the rider was a cowboy who wielded a lasso as he chased three cows across the hill. Howe was obviously making a connection between hunting and ranching, but the question is, whom did he intend the cowboy to represent?

While many white viewers would assume that the panels depicted a narrative about the Native American past being superseded by a new, white settler tradition of ranching, that is probably not the way Howe would have interpreted the imagery. For him, indigenous culture and ranching were intertwined. Over the course of the early twentieth century ranching became an increasingly common occupation for Native Americans of the upper plains.[38] In fact, it was practiced on Howe's family's own reservation. The appeal of Indian ranching can be seen in both children's literature and in Native American rodeos. For example, in 1947 Ann Clark, a friend of Howe's, published a bilingual children's book about a Native American ranching family called the *Singing Sioux Cowboy Reader.*[39] A popular book, it was reprinted many times, most recently in 1995. Howe had illustrated an earlier book by her, so he undoubtedly knew it.[40] Clark's fictitious family also enjoyed rodeos, and so did many other real-life Indian cowboys. Rodeos were

Figure 12a. Howe's Cowboy and Cattle Panel, 1948, Corn Palace main façade, Mitchell, South Dakota. Courtesy of Mitchell Area Historical Society; art reproduced courtesy of Mitchell Corn Palace and City of Mitchell.

Figure 12b. Howe's Indian and Buffalo Panel, 1948, Corn Palace main façade, Mitchell, South Dakota (postcard, author's collection). Art reproduced courtesy of Mitchell Corn Palace and City of Mitchell.

Stage (Two Panels)
The World's Only Corn Palace
Mitchell, S. D.

WELCOME

Figure 13. Howe's Interior Panels, 1948 Corn Palace, Mitchell, South Dakota (postcard, author's collection). Art reproduced courtesy of Mitchell Corn Palace and City of Mitchell.

common throughout the plains, and rodeo-like sporting events on reservations date as early as 1890. During the 1930s many Native American communities held annual rodeos, and by the 1950s exclusively Native rodeo associations had formed.[41] In light of all this, it cannot be assumed that Howe would have intended his corn palace cowboy panel to represent white culture. The similarity in the background, depicted in both panels, indicates the same place, but the juxtaposition of the Indian and the bison with the cowboy and the cattle indicates two time periods. Although white viewers may have assumed that white ranchers had replaced Indian hunters, in Howe's mind and that of his fellow Indian viewers, he showed that Native Americans had adapted to new conditions and continued to participate in shaping Midwestern history.

Howe's focus on the indigenous origin of the local economy also continued in the interior of the Palace (Figure 13). On the top of the proscenium, a "welcome" overstage mosaic featuring two cornucopias was retained from previous

years. It had been designed by local physician William Kearney. Howe updated it with the addition of descending side panels bearing Dakota symbols representing the rain cycle.[42] To the right of the stage Howe installed an image of two Indians kneeling before a dramatic landscape (Figure 14) and on the left (Figure 15) a "chief giving corn to a white man." Corner silhouettes represented a "white man's log cabin and Indian tepee," and a row of cornstalks lined the background.[43] How can this interior cycle be interpreted? Again there seems to be a juxtaposition of two different time periods. On the right, the Indians are alone, and the country is theirs to use as they will. On the left, an Indian of obvious authority welcomes the white man into his land and offers him the most sacred gift of all—corn—the product that will bring wealth to the territory and ultimately result in the celebratory Corn Palace that now bears testimony to that history. From a twenty-first-century point of view this panel seems troubling, as it glosses over the horrific history of white and Indian relations.

Another reading, however, suggests that Howe used the murals to assert the significance of Native culture and to remind white South Dakotans of what they owe to Native peoples. Unlike the 1887 Sioux City reporter who told a narrative of nomadic red men being replaced by white men planting cornfields, Howe asserts that the origin of corn lay in Indian cultivation. The resulting civilization was indebted to Indian skill, experience, and generosity.

Moreover, if we contrast the Longfellow version of the origin of corn with the Dakota version that Howe depicts, there are interesting differences. Hiawatha represented a version of the legend that, although informed by Ojibwe thinking, was modified by Longfellow to resonate with white people. In this version an Indian god has to die to be reborn as the corn plant. The echoes of that with Christian traditions of sacrifice and resurrection were often noted by corn palace commentators. When earlier corn muralists used images of Indians, it was often as a contrast between an Indian past and a white present. The Indians were a romantic image of a bygone era. Howe's version, however, emphasized a gift from nature (the nurturing lactating bison), Indian agency in cultivating the crop, and Indian generosity in sharing it. Finally, he also seems to be asserting a continuing presence of Indian participation. If the cowboy on the 1948 façade is an Indian, then Howe seems to be saying that Indians provide not only legends of the past but continue to be players in an ongoing history. In fact, by making the mosaics on the most prominent institution of the region and what was then the largest auditorium in South Dakota, he literally acted out that participation. And corn is at the center of it all.

Howe saw himself as an intermediary between cultures. He used the Corn Palace mosaics as a means of bringing people together and of helping to shape the public perception of both Native American people and the history of the region. Although he retired from working at the Palace nearly forty years ago, Howe's legacy remains important in the early twenty-first century. Six of his most successful panels remain installed inside the auditorium. It is also notable that one of Howe's Native American students, Arthur

Amiotte, was commissioned in 1981 to install a mosaic above the stage that focused on the "singular cycle of nature."

Amiotte used a visual vocabulary similar to that of his mentor. A bison sun flanked by a moon and star filled the top of the proscenium as the sun's rays cut across a rainbow. The life cycle of corn fills panels to the left and right of the stage with birds and raindrops in the background. Kernels fall to the earth on the far edges of the stage and are shown in progressive stages of growth. The centermost plants burst through clouds into the rainbow, thus marking the stage itself as the climax of farming (Figure 16).[44] Amiotte's painted plan included more colors than existed in the available corn, and it was thus reinterpreted by the white artist Calvin Schultz before installation. Although intended to be permanent,

Figure 14. Detail, Indians in landscape, Howe's Interior Panel, 1948 Corn Palace, Mitchell, South Dakota (postcard, author's collection). Art reproduced courtesy of Mitchell Corn Palace and City of Mitchell.

Figure 15. Detail, Indian chief offering corn gift, Howe's Interior Panel, 1948 Corn Palace, Mitchell, South Dakota (postcard, author's collection). Art reproduced courtesy of Mitchell Corn Palace and City of Mitchell.

Figure 16. Arthur Amiotte's 1981 overstage mosaic, Mitchell, South Dakota, Corn Palace. Courtesy of Mitchell Area Historical Society. Art reproduced courtesy of Mitchell Corn Palace and City of Mitchell.

Figure 17. Calvin Schultz, overstage mosaic, Mitchell, South Dakota, Corn Palace, 2004. Photograph by author. Art reproduced courtesy of Mitchell Corn Palace and City of Mitchell.

the Amiotte work was later replaced by one fully designed by Schultz. His design, refurbished with fresh corn, remains installed as of 2009 (Figure 17).[45] Although less visually complex than Amiotte's and more dichotomous than Howe's, it nonetheless addresses Native American subject matter and continues the dialogue that Howe began. It features red and white hands—clasping each other in a handshake of friendship—flanked by paired medallions depicting an Indian and a white person, a bison and a cow, a tepee and a cabin—the very imagery that Howe had introduced in 1948.

As the corn palaces bear witness, corn was and is basic to Midwestern prosperity. It was the basis for agribusiness, and its ties to Indians were both ancient and continuous in legend and popular imagery. The experience of Oscar Howe suggests that when we see Indians at the corn palaces, we may be looking at something far more complicated than simply a tale of white racial exploitation and appropriation projected onto a building façade. Rather, a contemporary reading that takes into consideration the point of view of the Indian participants suggests a more subtle tale of contested identities and histories that continues to unfold.

NOTES

1. For the history of the nineteenth-century cereal palaces, see Pamela H. Simpson, "Turn-of-the-Century Midwestern Corn Festivals: Kiosks and Crop Art as American Icons," *Arris* 14 (2003): 1–15; "Cereal Architecture: Late-Nineteenth-Century Grain Palaces and Crop Art," in *Building Environments: Perspectives in Vernacular Architecture* 10, eds. Kenneth A. Breisch and Alison K. Hoagland, 269–82 (Knoxville: University of Tennessee Press, 2005); Ruth S. Beitz, "Sioux City's Splendid Corn Palaces," *The Iowan Magazine* 9, no. 3 (February–March 1961): 18–19; John Ely Briggs, "The Sioux City Corn Palaces," *The Palimpsest* 44, no. 12 (1963): 549–62; Cynthia Elyce Rubin, "The Midwestern Corn Palaces: A 'Maize' of Detail and Wonder," *The Clarion* (1983): 24–31; Dorothy Schwieder and Patricia Swanson, "The Sioux City Corn Palaces," *Annals of Iowa* 41, no. 8 (Spring 1973): 1209–27.

2. Rogers Brubaker and Frederick Cooper, "Beyond 'Identity,'" *Theory and Society* 29, no. 1 (2000): 1–47.

3. A word about tribal names: The dominant Indian tribes of South Dakota are usually referred to by the general term "Sioux," even though the name may have had a derogatory connotation originally. Some controversy remains, but for lack of a better alternative the term is often accepted by both scholars and tribal members. The Sioux lived historically in the Dakotas, Minnesota, and Wisconsin, and the culture can be divided based on language into the Lakota, Dakota, and Nakota. These groups can be further divided into ten bands. Most precisely, Howe was born into the Yanktonai band of Nakota-speaking Sioux who lived east of the Missouri River. However, he evidently viewed the terms "Nakota" and "Dakota" as interchangeable and usually identified himself as "Dakota." For the sake of historical clarity in this paper, we will defer to his terms. See, for example, John R. Milton, *Oscar Howe* (Minneapolis: Dillon Press, 1972), 6.

4. James Henri Howard, "The Dakota or Sioux Indians: A Study in Human Ecology," *Reprints in Anthropology* 20, no. 2 (Lincoln, Neb.: J and L Reprint, 1980), 12. The author cited personal communication with the corn breeder George Will, in 1950.

5. This fact about the Mandan was known to white farmers and is reproduced, for example, in C. B. Heinemeyer, *When Corn Was King: A Historical Treatise on Corn Growing in Dakota* (Fargo, N.D.: Fargo Seed House, 1914), n.p. Heinemeyer took the quote from the following translation: Prince Maximilian of Wied, *Maximilian, Prince of Wied's Travels in the Interior of North America, 1832–1834*, ed. Reuben Gold Thwaites, trans. Hannibal Evans Lloyd, vol. 22–25 of *Early Western Travels, 1748–1846* (Cleveland: A. H. Clark Company, 1906), 275. The Mandan lived along the Missouri River, which is close to where Mitchell is today. They traded grain with the Dakota, so the varieties grown by the two tribes would have been almost identical. A discussion of this trade is included in Pekka Hämäläinen, "The Rise and Fall of Plains Indian Horse Cultures," *The Journal of American History* 90, no. 2 (2003): 855–56.

6. Paul F. Norton, *Latrobe, Jefferson, and the National Capitol* (New York: Garland, 1977), 220.

7. Candace Wheeler, ed., *Columbia's Emblem, Indian Corn* (Boston: Houghton, Mifflin and Co., 1893), iii–iv.

8. It was not until 1879 that the first fully illustrated American edition of the poem appeared. Another popular one followed in 1890, illustrated by Frederick Remington. Together they helped to inspire renewed

interest in the subject. This poem is perhaps most familiar to architectural historians through the sculptures *Nakoma* and *Nakomis* by Frank Lloyd Wright that were created in 1926, but the poem inspired innumerable other creative people during the nineteenth and twentieth centuries. See Cynthia D. Nickerson, "Artistic Interpretations of Henry Wadsworth Longfellow's *The Song of Hiawatha*, 1855–1900," *The American Art Journal* 16, no. 3 (Summer 1984): 49–77; Christopher P. Monkhouse, "Henry Wadsworth Longfellow and the Mississippi River: Forging a National Identity through the Arts," in *Currents of Change: Art and Life along the Mississippi River, 1850–1861,* ed. Jason T. Busch, Christopher Monkhouse, and Janet L. Whitmore, 140–84 (Minneapolis: Minneapolis Institute of Arts, 2004).

9. For a study of Longfellow's sources, see Stith Thompson, "The Indian Legend of Hiawatha," in *Publications of the Modern Language Association of America (PMLA)* 37, no. 1 (March 1922): 128–40.

10. *Sioux City Journal,* September 24, 1887, 3, printed the section of the poem recounting the origin of corn story. See *Mitchell Capital,* October 7, 1892, 7, for a description of a mural and *Exposition Souvenir,* October 6, 1893, 6, for a description of a Hiawatha painting in a cereal decorated frame. Mitchell Area Historical Society Collection at the Carnegie Resource Center.

11. *Sioux City Journal,* September 24, 1887, 3; also August 5, 1887, 3; and February 1, 1891, 3.

12. See, for example, Philip Joseph Deloria, *Playing Indian* (New Haven, Conn.: Yale University Press, 1998); Philip Joseph Deloria, *Indians in Unexpected Places* (Lawrence: University Press of Kansas, 2004); Rayna Green, "The Tribe Called Wannabee: Playing Indian in America and Europe," *Folklore* 99, no. 1 (1988): 30–55; Shari M. Huhndorf, *Going Native: Indians in the American Cultural Imagination* (Ithaca, N.Y.: Cornell University Press, 2001); S. Elizabeth Bird, ed., *Dressing in Feathers: The Construction of the Indian in American Popular Culture* (Boulder, Colo.: Westview Press, 1996); Carter Jones Meyer, and Diana Royer, eds., *Selling the Indian: Commercializing and Appropriating American Indian Cultures* (Tucson: University of Arizona Press, 2001). For a major treatment of stereotyped depictions of Indians in art and literature, see Robert F. Berkhofer, *The White Man's Indian: Images of the American Indian from Columbus to the Present* (New York: Knopf, 1978).

13. Simpson, "Turn-of-the-Century Midwestern Corn Festivals," 1–2. Originally documented in *Souvenir—Atchison Corn Carnival 1902* (Atchison, Kans., *Atchison Daily Globe,* 1902), 3 and 25, pamphlet in the collection of the Atchison Public Library.

14. *Sioux City Journal,* September 17, 1887, 6; October 5, 1887, 1, for description of the "Squaw Race." The voyeuristic attitude of the reporter is clearly evident, as he noted that "they shed enough of their wardrobes to give them easy locomotion, a few being without stockings and all without shoes."

15. *Sioux City Journal,* October 9, 1887, 1, notes "The committee were pleased with the Indian exhibit in the Palace and want to encourage these aborigines in their efforts to flow with the tide of civilization and become useful people instead of savages," and October 13, 1887, 1, describes President Cleveland's visit to the Corn Palace and his astonishment at the Indian exhibit and the size of the ears of corn they had grown as well as the "pretty designs . . . all the work of the untutored savage."

16. *Mitchell Capital,* September 30, 1892, 4.

17. *Mitchell Capital,* September 26, 1893, 2, and *Davidson County Gazette,* n.d., clipping in Mitchell Area Historical Society files, Carnegie Resource Center.

18. *Sioux City Journal,* October 5, 1887, 1.

19. Leonard A. Carlson, *Indians, Bureaucrats, and Land: The Dawes Act and the Decline of Indian Farming* (Westport, Conn.: Greenwood Press, 1981).

20. Frank Pommersheim, *Broken Ground and Flowing Water* (Rosebud, S.D.: Sinte Gleska College Press, 1977).

21. *Sioux City Journal,* October 8, 1887, 1, recounts an incident where the Corn Palace organizers had planned on having an Indian War Dance as part of the entertainments, but they were disappointed when "a telegram was received from the war department refusing to let the Indians give an exhibition dance." They also noted that they could not explain why the government would refuse to let the "noble red man" give "samples of his savage life." Forbidding Indian dances was government policy, and it would be reinforced in 1890 after the Ghost Dance movement and the massacre at Wounded Knee. See L. G. Moses, *Wild West Shows and the Images of American Indians, 1883–1933* (Albuquerque: University of New Mexico Press, 1996), 104–7.

22. *Sioux City Journal,* October 5, 1887, 1.

23. Moses, *Wild West Shows,* 103.

24. Ibid., 210–11.

25. Such Indian adaptation of agricultural festivals for their own purposes should not be surprising, given that in this era identity and forms of entertainment were being rethought in profound ways. See the essays on British culture, for example, in Eric J. Hobsbawm, and Terence O. Ranger, eds. *The Invention of Tradition* (Cambridge: Cambridge University Press, 1983). In the case of Native American culture, powwows are one such example. Although powwows have roots in longstanding traditions, they took on their modern form in the late nineteenth century. A cottage industry also arose, particularly in the upper Midwest, through which Native women made beaded garments and objects for the Wild West Shows, Red Men's fraternal lodges, and entertainment fairs. Much of the "traditional" clothing from the upper plains displayed in ethnographic and art museums today was made in the late nineteenth century for these purposes. For a discussion of Plains Indian identity at this time, including the status of vaguely provenanced museum objects, see Marsha C. Bol, "Defining Lakota Tourist Art, 1880–1915," in *Unpacking Culture: Art and Commodity in Colonial and Postcolonial Worlds,* ed. Ruth B. Phillips and Christopher Burghard Steiner (Berkeley: University of California Press, 1999), 214–28.

26. See *The Mitchell Capital,* July through October 7, 1892 for daily items about the corn palace plans, construction, and decoration, as well as Rohe's participation. The Mitchell Area Historical Society collection on the Corn Palace is housed at the Carnegie Resource Center. Also see Mitchell Chamber of Commerce, *A Year by Year History of the World's Only Corn Palace,* 5th ed. (Mitchell, S.D.: Educator Supply Co., 1957); Bob Karolevitz, *An Historic Sampler of Davison County* (Virginia Beach, Va.: The Donning Co., 1993); Robert Schutt, *The Corn Palace Story* (Sioux Falls: Dakota News, 1976).

27. *Sioux Falls Press,* n.d., 1892, clipping in Mitchell Area Historical Society Corn Palace Collection, Carnegie Resource Center.

28. Numerous journal articles have been published about individual buildings designed by Rapp and Rapp, but the best overview of their work remains a self-published monograph. C. W. Rapp and Geo. L. Rapp, *The Recent Work of C. W. And Geo. L. Rapp* (Chicago: n.p., 1927). The firm's blueprints for the Corn Palace are housed in the Mitchell City Hall.

29. The external appearance of the Corn Palace was radically reinterpreted by the local architect Floyd Kings (son of the city's first palace builder Andrew Kings) in 1937. Hired to add an annex onto the Palace to serve as the city hall, armory, and recreation center, he designed a contrasting Art Deco style structure. At the same time, Kings transformed the original place by adding Moorish domes, minarets, and awnings. Thus, Howe inherited in 1948 a prominent building made up of a hodgepodge of styles. "Mitchell Citizens Will Vote on Bond Issue for New Armory Building Tuesday," *Mitchell Daily Republican,* June 18, 1937, 1; "Moorish Architecture Dominates Re-Modeled Corn Palace," *Mitchell Gazette,* September 23, 1937, 1.

30. For a history of Oscar Howe at the Mitchell Corn Palace, see Travis E. Nygard, "Oscar Howe and the Metaphorical Monarchy of Maize: Indigenism and Power in the Mitchell Corn Palace Panels, 1948–1971," M.A. thesis, University of Pittsburgh, 2005.

31. For material on Howe, see the Oscar Howe Archives in the Herman P. Chilson Collection of Western Americana in the I. D. Weeks Library at the University of South Dakota, Vermillion, and the Dakota Discovery Museum, which houses the Oscar Howe Gallery in Mitchell, South Dakota; see also Frederick J. Dockstader, ed., *Oscar Howe: A Retrospective Exhibition: Catalogue Raisonné* (Tulsa, Okla.: Thomas Gilcrease Museum Association, 1982); John R. Millon, *Oscar Howe,* 1972; Robert Pennington, *Oscar Howe: Artist of the Sioux* (Sioux Falls, S.D.: Dakota Territory Centennial Commission, 1961); Mark White, "Oscar Howe and the Transformation of Native American Art," *American Indian Art Magazine* 23, no. 1 (1997): 36–43. On Dorothy Dunn's endeavors, see Bruce Bernstein and W. Jackson Rushing, *Modern by Tradition: American Indian Painting in the Studio Style* (Santa Fe: Museum of New Mexico Press, 1995), Bill Anthes, *Native Moderns: American Indian Painting, 1940–1960* (Durham, N.C.: Duke University Press, 2006), 142–70.

32. His other major mural cycle was commissioned for the municipal auditorium in Mobridge, South Dakota. Julius Skaug, *The Mobridge Murals: Mobridge Municipal Auditorium* (Mobridge, S.D.: Mobridge Tribune, after 1951).

33. Howe, "Indian Designer Makes Statement," *Mitchell Gazette,* September 16, 1948, 1. Later, in 1977, Oscar Howe was asked by the of the Institute of American Indian Studies' South Dakota Oral History Project to compose a series of questions about his life and

work and then to answer those questions. One of his questions focused on the Corn Palace, and he noted that he had wanted to design panels for it for ten years before he was hired. Oscar Howe interviewed by Oscar Howe, July 12, 1977. Research data obtained through the archives of the South Dakota Oral History Center, Institute of American Indian Studies, University of South Dakota, Vermillion, South Dakota. American Indian Research Project Collection, Tape 1044.

34. The complete letter is reproduced in Jeanne Snodgrass King, "The Preeminence of Oscar Howe," in *Oscar Howe: A Retrospective Exhibition: Catalogue Raisonné,* ed. Frederick J. Dockstader (Tulsa, Okla.: Thomas Gilcrease Museum Association, 1982), 19. A lengthier analytical treatment of this shift is by Mark White, "Oscar Howe and the Transformation of Native American Art," 36–43.

35. Robert Pennington, *Oscar Howe: Artist of the Sioux* (Sioux Falls, S.D.: Dakota Territory Centennial Commission, 1961), 32–33. Pennington quotes Howe explaining that, "Working with whole and half ears of corn necessitates making straight lines in the designs" (33). He attributes the quote to "Grandmother's Finger Painting First Instruction of South Dakota Artist," *The Mitchell [S.D.] Daily Republic,* December 14, 1951, n.p. Also see John R. Milton, *Oscar Howe* (Minneapolis: Dillon Press, 1972), 36.

36. Oscar Howe, "Indian Designer Makes Statement," *Mitchell [SD] Gazette,* September 16, 1948, 1. "Corn Palace Decorations," in *The 1948 Corn Palace Revue,* program from festival held in Mitchell, South Dakota, September 20–25, 1948, n.p. Mitchell Area Historical Society archives, Carnegie Research Center, Corn Palace Collection. Oscar Howe, "Story by Artist from Sioux Indian Tribe: Origin of Corn—A Sioux Indian Legend" (n.d.), typed statement available in the City Hall in Nebraska City. The Nebraska City *Origin of Corn* painting was listed on Howe's resume as a mural, but it is actually a large framed oil painting. The watercolor sketch for it was published by Marsha V. Gallagher, "Oscar Howe," in *Fifty Favorites from Joslyn Art Museum* (Omaha, Neb.: Joslyn Art Museum, 1994). The Dakota origin of corn myth is recounted by Garrick Mallery, *Picture-Writing of the American Indians* (New York: Dover, 1972), 290–91. He notes there are several versions of it. The one he discusses states that a beautiful woman appeared to the Dakota and told them she was "the White-Buffalo-Cow" and that she would spill her milk all over the earth. She gave them

four kernels of maize, one red, one black, one white, and one yellow, then disappeared over the hill where they followed to find a herd of buffalo.

37. Hämäläinen, "The Rise and Fall of Plains Indian Horse Cultures," 845, paragraph 24.

38. Peter Iverson, *When Indians Became Cowboys: Native Peoples and Cattle Ranching in the American West* (Norman: University of Oklahoma Press, 1994), 52–84, 138, 140–47, 157–66.

39. The book is written in English and the Lakota dialect. Ann Nolan Clark, *Singing Sioux Cowboy Reader* (Lawrence, Kans.: U.S. Indian Service, 1947). This book is discussed and pages of it are reproduced by Peter Iverson, *When Indians Became Cowboys,* 182–86.

40. Howe illustrated Clark's, *Bringer of the Mystery Dog* (Lawrence, Kans.: U.S. Department of the Interior, Bureau of Indian Affairs, Haskell Institute, 1943).

41. Morgan Baillargeon and Leslie Tepper, *Legends of Our Times: Native Cowboy Life* (Vancouver: University of British Columbia Press, 1998).

42. This panel would have appealed to the populace, as Howe's WPA mural in the dome of the Carnegie Library in Mitchell created in 1940 also focused on rain. George Agogino and Heidi Howe, "Oscar Howe, Sioux Artist," *Institute of Indian Studies: Occasional Papers,* no. 1 (1959), n.p.

43. "Corn Palace Decorations," n.p.

44. Writing about Arthur Amiotte includes: Janet Catherine Berlo and Arthur Amiotte, *Arthur Amiotte: Collages, 1988–2006* (Santa Fe, N.M.: Exhibition catalog from the Wheelwright Museum of the American Indian, 2006); John Day, ed., *Arthur Amiotte, Retrospective Exhibition: Continuity and Diversity* (Pine Ridge, S.D.: The Heritage Center, Inc., Red Cloud Indian School, 2001); Jennifer Vigil, "Drawing Past, Present and Future: The Legacy of the Plains Indian Graphic Tradition in the Works of Arthur Amiotte" (PhD diss., University of Iowa, 2004). For Amiotte's relationship to Howe, see especially John Day's essay "Arthur Amiotte and Oscar Howe: Sympathy and Divergence," in *Arthur Amiotte: Retrospective Exhibition,* 19–24. On the mosaic itself, see "Corn Palace Mural," *Mitchell Daily Republic,* July 14, 1981, 6.

45. Upon reinstallation the design was altered by making the medallions larger, but the content and composition of those medallions has been unaltered. On Schultz's art and biography, see Paula Guhin, *The King of Corn, Cal Schultz: Having the Times of His Life* (Aberdeen, S.D.: Prairie Home Press, 2002).

LILLIAN MAKEDA

A Fly in the Amber

Route 66 Architecture at Petrified Forest National Monument

Located in eastern Arizona, Petrified Forest National Park is renowned for its spectacular geography and outstanding paleontological resources. The area was set aside as one of the first national monuments created by President Theodore Roosevelt after the passage of the Antiquities Act of 1906.[1] Living trees are few and far between in the rolling landscape of this bleak and desolate region, where the remains of ancient forests endure as some of the most important deposits of petrified wood in the world (Figure 1).

The arrival of sightseers by way of the Thirty-Fifth Parallel Transcontinental Railroad Line and the National Old Trails Road (later to become Route 66) prompted both the National Park Service and private enterprise to develop architecture that would frame the touristic experience of Petrified Forest. Diverging objectives produced sharply contrasting designs for buildings. The National Park Service favored the Spanish–Pueblo Revival style from 1929 to 1942, and the International Style from 1958 through 1965.[2] Private enterprise, along Route 66, built commercial vernacular buildings that epitomized the "flamboyant hucksterism" often found in contemporary roadside architecture.[3] The Park Service at Petrified Forest viewed these types of ventures as "undesirable" and worked assiduously to remove them from the landscape. The most contentious business site was known as the Painted Desert Park or, alternatively, the Lion Farm, a small operation that sold gasoline, souvenirs, and snacks. Between the late 1950s and mid-1960s, archetypal examples of each of these three styles—Spanish-Pueblo Revival, the

International Style, and commercial vernacular—comprised the only buildings on a plateau overlooking the Painted Desert in the northern part of the monument and were located a short distance from each other (Figure 2). This striking architectural juxtaposition would have been further heightened by the area's flat, barren terrain.

In 1930, the National Park Service embarked on a lengthy campaign to take control of the architecture in and around Petrified Forest and eliminate the Lion Farm. The built environment of the park as it appears today reflects a plan conceived exclusively by the Park Service, which finally triumphed after a protracted battle that pitted federal and state governments against small-scale entrepreneurs who sought to make a living near the Painted Desert. The conflict at Petrified Forest represents only one instance of what has been an ongoing endeavor to assert government influence over the property within and around national parks and monuments. On a national level, these efforts have met with varying degrees of success, but when it came to Petrified Forest, the Park Service ultimately prevailed.

Petrified Forest National Monument
Accounts of petrified wood in eastern Arizona began to receive wide distribution after the completion of the Atlantic and Pacific railway line in 1883.[4] The railroad furnished the primary means of approach for over thirty years, and the area became one of several attractions that would be packaged by the Atchison, Topeka, and Santa Fe as "the American Southwest." Charles Lummis, famous for *Mesa, Cañon, and Pueblo* and other publications describing his travels in the region,

Figure 1. Petrified Forest National Monument, 1946. From 1906 to 1932, the boundaries of Petrified Forest National Monument were located south of the Thirty-fifth Parallel Transcontinental Railway Line; most visitors disembarked at Adamana or Holbrook. The development of Route 66 was followed by the addition of the Painted Desert to the monument in 1932. Detail from a map located in the Petrified Forest National Park Archives.

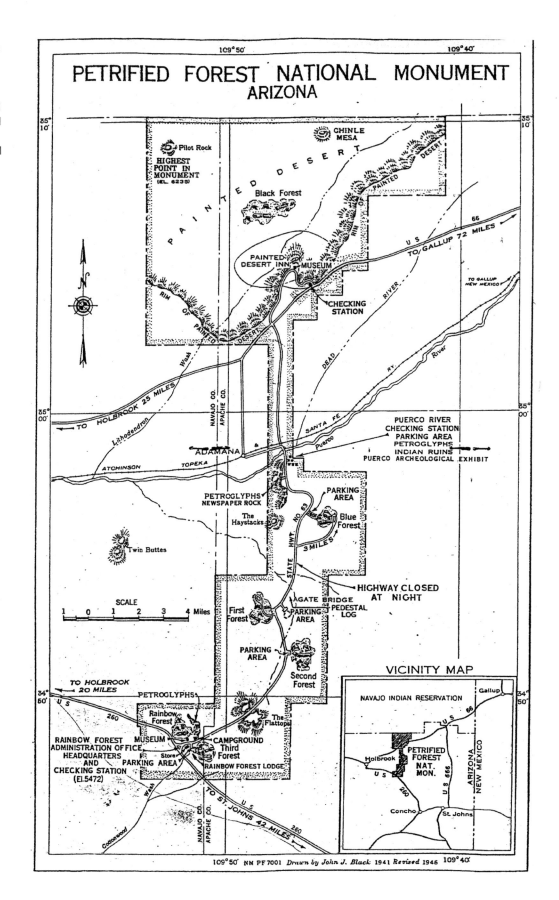

helped popularize the beauty of Petrified Forest National Monument. A 1912 article published in *Santa Fe Employee's Magazine* exclaimed:

And the sight of them! The Titan trunks lying as they were felled by some unknown cataclysm, their chameleon chips paving an area half the size of the state of Rhode Island and shimmering at sunrise or at sunset as Sinbad never saw; their broken cross sections so radiant, bark and fiber, as no man ever before beheld outside his dreams![5]

Tourism at Petrified Forest steadily increased during the early twentieth century as automobile travel offered visitors convenient access to the area. The National Old Trails Road, one of the first transcontinental highways in America, was mapped by 1913 and followed a route from New York to Los Angeles that passed only eighteen miles north of the monument. By 1926, the Old Trails Road had merged with a federal system of highways and became known by a new name: Route 66.

A presidential proclamation in 1932 authorized a dramatic expansion that doubled the size of Petrified Forest National Monument to include a part of Arizona's Painted Desert. The Painted Desert is famous for its colorful landforms tinted in shades of pink, purple, green, blue and brown; the newly added area also contains "the Black Forest," notable for its massive "logs" of dark-colored petrified wood. The acquisition of the Painted Desert in 1932 made Petrified Forest National Monument the only unit in the National Park system to span Route 66.

The Development of the Lion Farm

The most problematic Route 66 roadside business for the Park Service was the Lion Farm.[6] Although originally situated just outside of Petrified Forest, the 1932 proclamation enclosed Section 2, T 19N, R 24E, the site of the Lion Farm, within the boundaries of the monument.

Harry E. "Indian" Miller, a prominent figure in the annals of Arizona Route 66 history, leased the section from the state of Arizona in 1925 while working at Fort Two Guns, another Route 66 business located between Flagstaff and

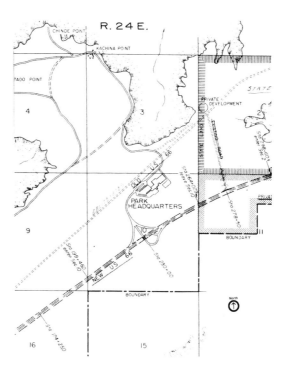

R. 24 E.

Figure 2. The Painted Desert area of Petrified Forest National Monument, with section outlines (each section measures one square mile), January 1959. The Lion Farm is identified in Section 2 as "Private Development," and the Painted Desert Inn is located at Kachina Point. The Painted Desert Community was constructed on the site of "Park Headquarters," although its final plan was modified from what is depicted here. The spur road (indicated as "Existing Road") provided access to the Lion Farm from the new alignment of Route 66 from 1955 to 1958. The map has been marked up by Superintendent Fred Fagergren to show the obliteration of the spur road and the stretch of Route 66 within the monument. Detail of a larger map in "The Superior Court of the State of Arizona in and for the County of Apache, Transcript of Proceedings—*Painted Desert Park, Inc. v. State Land Department*, Case nos. 3603 and 3661," Courthouse, St. Johns, Arizona, July 10, 1961, 199–200. Courtesy of Clerk of the Court, Apache County, St. Johns, Arizona.

Winslow, Arizona. Within a year or two, he had joined with his nephews Paul and William Jacobs to construct the Lion Farm.[7] By 1930, Miller had left to open another Route 66 endeavor, the Cave of the Seven Devils near the Arizona–New Mexico state line, and his sister Julia Miller (Paul and William Jacobs's mother) had taken over as proprietor. The main buildings were situated on the north side of Route 66 facing south toward the highway; the sloping precipice that forms the edge of the Painted Desert dropped sharply to the rear (Figure 3).[8] Because the Lion Farm was positioned on the rim of a small peninsula protruding into the Desert, it was ideally configured to take advantage of the area's dramatic scenery and offered an impressive view.

The Lion Farm was one of thousands of wayside stands that proliferated along American roads during the 1920s.[9] The entrepreneurs who built these establishments typically opted for plain, simple vernacular structures; conspicuous signage compensated for any austerity in design.[10] Cheap, readily available materials were characteristic, and in many cases, other types of buildings or recycled items were modified for commercial use. By the middle of the decade, as automobile ownership became firmly

Figure 3. During the 1930s, the buildings at the Lion Farm were laid out on a U-shaped plan that opened onto Route 66, as shown in this photo dating from circa 1933. The main buildings, viewed from the east side of the Lion Farm's filling station, included, from far left, the Painted Desert Observatory, store, hexagonal "Native-American" structure, and zoo. Courtesy of the Petrified Forest National Park Archives.

entrenched in American culture, a distinctive roadside architecture began to appear.[11] As historian Chester Liebs has observed, the crucible for these experiments was located in exurbia, where design conventions and legal constraints were largely absent.[12] The Lion Farm, constructed in the late 1920s, was representative of the transition from sign-based advertising to the use of buildings to market roadside ventures.

The architecture of the Lion Farm was carnivalesque and "quite colorful."[13] By 1934, the operation included a two-story viewing platform, a store, a polygonal building with conical roof, a set of restrooms painted in broad stripes, several small wooden cabins, and a zoo entered through a towering gate painted with pictures of wild animals and topped with a large American flag. The viewing platform, the roof of the polygonal building, and the gate to the zoo served to add vertical, visually arresting elements to the site's architecture. The buildings were arranged in a U-shape to form a plaza adjoining Route 66. A small Conoco filling station stood within the plaza, close to the road (Figure 4). Fences and walls were covered with signs, large and small, promoting the remarkable adventures and tasty refreshments that lay in store for the road-weary traveler.

The curio shop at the Lion Farm offered a variety of items, including Navajo blankets, pottery, petrified wood jewelry, and art made from the sands of the Painted Desert.[14] Signage nearby advertised groceries and food items, including "Hot Coffee and Sandwiches," "Ice Cold Beer," and "Fresh Jersey Milk" and urged travelers to "Try Our Hot Bar-B-Q Sandwiches."[15] The store building had dirt floors and was constructed from railroad ties, an inexpensive and easily obtainable material.

The corners of the polygonal building adjoining the store were decorated with roundels of petrified wood, giving the impression that it was made of petrified wood logs.[16] Chunks of petrified wood were embedded in the earth-colored stucco covering its walls and the walls of the store. The Navajo reservation directly abuts the northern boundary of Petrified Forest National Monument and the polygonal footprint of the building echoed the Navajo *hooghan,* which is traditionally polygonal or round in plan. The roof may also have been intended to evoke a teepee (teepee village camps for tourists had appeared in the National Park System as early as 1914 at Glacier National Park).[17] With a roof adorned by a swastika (recognizable as a Native American symbol during this period), it seems likely that the architect was attempting to create the impression of an exotic, if not entirely authentic Native American dwelling. Over the years, the

Figure 4. The filling station at the Lion Farm, looking northwest from Route 66, circa 1933. One of the Lion Farm's tourist cabins is visible in the background on the left, and Petrified Forest National Monument can be seen in the distance. From Superintendent Charles J. Smith, "Report on Complaint of Julia G. Miller," August 5, 1933. Courtesy of the Petrified Forest National Park Archives.

Figure 5. The public restrooms and Painted Desert Observatory at the Lion Farm, looking north, 1934. These structures were situated on the northwest side of the store building. From H. D. Moulton, "Petrified Forest National Monument, Arizona, Chas. J. Smith, Superintendent, Official Conduct and Related Matters. Favorable Report" (November 24, 1934); RG 79, Central Classified Files, 1933–49; National Archives and Records Administration, College Park, Maryland.

space inside served both as a sleeping area and for storage.

By 1934, overnight accommodations were available in a row of cabins bounding the west side of the Lion Farm. Behind the store, toward the edge of the bluff, was the "Painted Desert Observatory," a two-story, open-framed tower equipped with a telescope (Figure 5). Patrons of the Lion Farm could climb the stairs to a balustraded platform and obtain a panoramic view of the landscape. Public restrooms could be found nearby; to the east of the tower was the enclosed cistern.

The zoo was located on the east side of the Lion Farm. Its corrugated iron enclosure was covered with hand-lettered advertisements that made much of the thrills and excitement to be found within. Signs painted around the parking area played heavily on "the baby lions" and lured travelers with the promise that they could be photographed while holding a lion cub "for free." The fence on the south side of the zoo

Figure 6. The zoo at the Lion Farm, looking north from Route 66, 1934. From H. D. Moulton, "Petrified Forest National Monument, Arizona, Chas. J. Smith, Superintendent, Official Conduct and Related Matters. Favorable Report" (November 24, 1934); RG 79, Central Classified Files, 1933–49; National Archives and Records Administration, College Park, Maryland.

Figure 7. The interior of the zoo at the Lion Farm, looking east, 1934. The petrified logs that are visible here probably formed the Lion Farm's "petrified forest." From H. D. Moulton, "Petrified Forest National Monument, Arizona, Chas. J. Smith, Superintendent, Official Conduct and Related Matters. Favorable Report" (November 24, 1934); RG 79, Central Classified Files, 1933–49; National Archives and Records Administration, College Park, Maryland.

along Route 66 read "Painted Desert Park Zoo" and "Mountain Lion Farm" in huge characters intended to catch the eyes of passing motorists (Figure 6).

The tallest structure at the Lion Farm was the gateway to the zoo. For 25 cents, visitors could gain entrance and have a look inside (Figure 7). In August 1933, they would have encountered "One antelope fawn, two eagles, one bobcat, one coyote, one fox, one mountain lion, one mongrel dog (similar to [a] German Police Dog), one house cat, and two kittens."[18] During various periods the zoo also exhibited Gila monsters, an owl, badgers, and pigs.[19] A sign leaning by the gate read "Entrance, Zoo and Petrified Forest." The interior of the zoo was scattered with pieces of petrified wood and there is little doubt that several large petrified stumps formed the purported "forest." The Lion Farm also had two or three stuffed horses, saddled up and frozen in a "bucking bronco" position. Visitors could climb on top for a dramatic photo opportunity (Figure 8).

The geography of the Painted Desert also allowed the residents of the Lion Farm to design a unique architectural typology known as a "chocey." According to oral sources, a chocey was a "man-made cave" carved into the top of a precipice. The bentonite clay that comprises the Painted Desert is soft and could be easily removed. To construct a chocey, all that was necessary was to dig enough earth to form a usable space, cover the opening with some kind of roof, and add a runnel to divert water. One such structure, located behind the zoo, was used to keep horsemeat fresh for the consumption of both the mountain lions and the Miller family. Alvin Hermetet, Julia Miller's boyfriend and an employee at the Lion Farm, also lived in a chocey to the west of the property. Hermetet excavated several rooms, covered the top of his dwelling with car doors, and even installed a hinged door at the entrance.[20]

The appearance of the Lion Farm forged a connection with passing motorists through the use of iconic imagery "embedded in the public's mind by dime novels, Wild West shows, travel brochures, postcards, stereopticon views, advertising, museums, and finally, the movies."[21] The Native American–influenced architecture and the "Wild Animals of the Southwest" were highly evocative for many Euro-Americans. By incorporating these elements into the Lion Farm, the builders implemented a strategy that was becoming increasingly discernible along roadsides across the country: the use of historic references that would resonate with potential customers.

The Lion Farm Becomes a Problem
The federal government began to crack down on roadside businesses around Petrified Forest in 1930, and documents indicate that the Lion Farm became a principal target.[22] The response of the Park Service can be seen as part of a larger movement that emerged during the 1920s, a decade during which the number of automobiles in the United States tripled, and the proliferation of cars drew thousands of entrepreneurs with an eye to a profit.[23] The businesses that sprang up along American roads frequently contained architectural features that gave offense to so-called "refined" sensibilities. By the late 1920s, the National Council for the Protection of Roadside Beauty was well established, the largest of

Figure 8. Gloria Olsen, age ten, on a stuffed "bucking bronco" at the Lion Farm, circa 1939. Courtesy of Gloria Olsen Slipher.

several organizations committed to rectifying the appearance of roadside landscapes.[24]

The problem was that wayside businesses frequently had to market themselves to customers who were traveling at high speeds. The need to catch the eye quickly and make a strong impression was inescapable. Large, garish signs and unusual (sometimes outrageous) looking buildings were becoming commonplace, and these structures were commonly inflected toward the road, making them even harder to avoid. Many of the 3 million people who joined roadside beautification groups during the 1920s were looking for a peaceful, uninterrupted respite from the stimulations and distractions of the city.[25] The architecture that greeted them as they drove out into the countryside often offered the very antithesis of the experience they were seeking.

In the spring of 1931, B. B. Craig of the U.S. General Land Office visited the Painted Desert north of Petrified Forest National Monument in order to evaluate its potential as a federally sponsored recreational area. In a report filed on May 7, he recommended that the government acquire a parcel of land along the southern boundary of Route 66, which had "no scenic value," but which would be useful "for the purpose of eliminating 'hot dog' stands and the like, that so often mar entrances to National Monuments."[26] Craig's disdain for certain types of roadside architecture was echoed a month later by Superintendent Charles "White Mountain" Smith. On June 8, Smith wrote a passionate letter to National Park Service Director Horace Albright criticizing businesses that were profiting from selling petrified wood. According to Smith,

> The petrified wood from the Black Forest is being rapidly carted away by irresponsible persons who have set up shacks along US Highway No. 66, which extends east and west a few miles south of this area, and the wood is then peddled to tourists for what ever amount that can be obtained. In many cases there are several tons scattered around these shanties, with a sign on the road labeled "Petrified Forest" and in some cases visitors actually believe that they have seen the Petrified Forest National Monument.[27]

It was understandable that Smith and his confrères at the National Park Service would be concerned about the Route 66 landscape. By the early 1930s, Route 66 had become one of the most important cross-country routes in America. Westbound travelers encountered the Lion Farm about two miles before the northern Park Service entrance to Petrified Forest. The proximity of the Lion Farm linked it to the monument and colored the initial impression of thousands of motorists.

The federal government also viewed the Lion Farm as detracting from the emotional experience of viewing the Painted Desert. Made up of badlands, devoid of vegetation and characterized by rolling landforms tinted in variegated layers, the Painted Desert possesses a stark quality bordering on the sublime. Its unusual and even unearthly appearance affords the visitor a sense of the fantastic. As part of the "American Southwest," the Painted Desert and Petrified Forest belong to a group of dramatic landscapes, "the gallery of the extraordinary," that many viewed

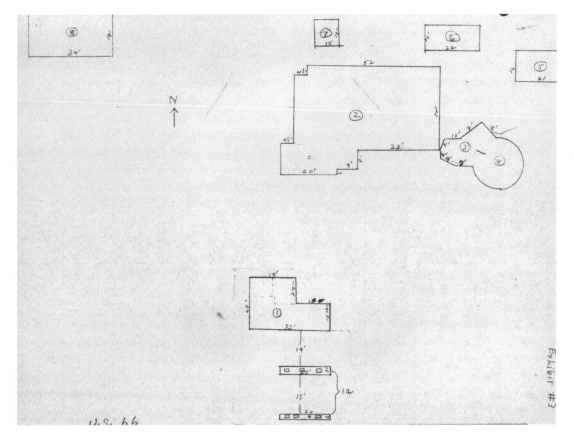

Figure 9. Plot plan of the Lion Farm, 1956. "1" is the filling station with two gasoline pump islands in front and restrooms at the rear; "2" is the main store building; "3" is the hexagonal "Native-American" structure; "4" is the stone hogan; "5" is the east dormitory; "6" is the cistern house; "7" is the Painted Desert Observatory; and "8" is the west dormitory. Route 66 is located along the bottom of the plan. From Larry Burke, "Appraisal of Sec. 2, T19N, R24E, G&SRB&M for the United States of America," (December 14, 1956). Courtesy of the Petrified Forest National Park Archives.

Figure 10a. The main buildings at the Lion Farm, looking east, 1934. From H. D. Moulton, "Petrified Forest National Monument, Arizona, Chas. J. Smith, Superintendent, Official Conduct and Related Matters. Favorable Report" (November 24, 1934); RG 79, Central Classified Files, 1933–49; National Archives and Records Administration, College Park, Maryland.

Figure 10b. The main buildings at the Lion Farm, looking east, 1956. The Painted Desert Observatory is visible on the left but is no longer singled out as an attraction. The café has been added onto the southwest side of the store, a vestibule extends from the main entrance, and the zoo has been replaced by a stone hogan. From J. Leslie Hansen, "An Appraisal of the Value of the Property Known as Painted Desert Park, 26 Miles East of Holbrook on U.S. Highway 66, Apache County, Arizona" (December 14, 1956). Courtesy of the Petrified Forest National Park Archives.

as part of America's national identity.[28] Unfettered by signs of modernity, the Painted Desert could furnish the setting for an imagined past and become the locus of historic fantasy. Mythic associations with the presettlement period of the American West could be more easily entertained. The presence of the Lion Farm, however, eliminated any possibility for romantic flights of reverie. Photographs dating from the 1950s clearly show the presence of two outhouses on the slopes of the Painted Desert that were almost certainly visible from within the monument.[29]

The Redevelopment of the Lion Farm

Around 1940, the Lion Farm began a new phase when Julia Miller transferred ownership to a group of local businessmen that included her son Charles H. Jacobs. Mrs. Miller, then in her seventieth year, moved south to Phoenix where she took over management of an apartment complex.[30] Jacobs and his partners subsequently expanded the operation with a series of new buildings that were likely motivated by both aesthetic and financial concerns (Figure 9).[31] In his monthly report for April 1941, Superintendent Thomas Whitcraft, who had replaced Charles Smith in 1940, remarked upon the construction activity at the Lion Farm. According to Whitcraft, the property "has had many improvements added to the minor development that existed on Route 66. It is understood that the new managers intend to spend approximately $50,000.00 on improvements during the year."[32]

Additions to the Lion Farm store included a café and a vestibule; the café opened for business during the autumn of 1951 (Figure 10). The tire

Figure 11. The interior of the Lion Farm, early 1950s. The front entrance is located on the left, and owner Albert Tietjen is pictured on the right. The retail space was L-shaped and offered refreshments as well as a wide variety of souvenir items. Courtesy of Leonora Tietjen Wilhelm.

racks inside the store were also removed, and the interior was wholly devoted to offering a variety of souvenirs and refreshments (Figure 11). "Tourist-quality" items included tomahawks, drums, various ceramics, baskets, decorative gourds, Indian "peace pipes," lamps with Southwest-themed shades, statues of Jesus and the Virgin Mary, specimens of Desert Rose (a geological formation), leather jackets, belts, footwear, vials of colored sand, books about Native Americans, sunglasses, framed pictures, postcards, film, souvenir decals, and, of course, pieces of petrified wood. Some of the silver jewelry and Navajo rugs were significantly higher in quality than the tourist knick-knacks.[33] Beer, soft drinks, candy, and ice cream were also available, as was a View-master machine that made pictures "come to life" in full color and three dimensions.

Part of the new construction at the Lion Farm linked the venture with the vernacular architecture of local Native Americans. Around 1940, the zoo was replaced with a round hogan made of stone (known in Navajo as a *hooghan nímazí*). Adjoining the hogan in front of the Lion Farm store was a Navajo *chaha'oh,* a type of brush arbor that shaded the entrance.[34] Over the course of his life, Charles H. Jacobs, coowner of the Lion Farm, was to own three different

Route 66 businesses in eastern Arizona, including the Navajo Indian Village and the Painted Desert Tower, all of which employed the use of a *hooghan nímazí* and a *chaha'oh.*[35] These two structures harmonized with the cultural geography of the Lion Farm and formed an architectural signature for Jacobs. Like the Painted Desert Observatory and the zoo, they were also almost certainly intended to attract attention and increase business.

Other additions to the Lion Farm during this era included a new filling station and new restrooms. Two rectangular dormitories were built to the east and west sides of the store, and two small tourist cabins could be found over the highway, on the south side of Route 66. Photographs show a strong likeness to the cabins that were present during the 1930s, and it is possible that these structures were hauled across Route 66 and relocated. Various outbuildings, piles of refuse, and abandoned vehicles were also situated across the highway within Section 2. The supporting timbers of the Painted Desert Observatory had been enclosed by the 1950s, and the tower became a storage space after the structure became too dangerous to climb.[36]

Park Service leadership closely monitored the possibility of further expansion at the Lion Farm. During 1950–1951, the owners introduced plans to add as many as one hundred cabins and install new facilities. Reports from the superintendent's office followed these developments almost on a monthly basis.[37]

With the elimination of the zoo, a large viewing area opened up to the east along the edge of the Painted Desert rim (Figure 12). The Lion Farm now afforded convenient access to the Painted Desert and provided a popular option to the monument for many travelers passing through the area. A 1954 Park Service boundary study concluded, "It is probably true that there are many persons who stop and view the Painted Desert from the rim in State Section 2 who would not take the time to drive the loop road in order to see the Painted Desert from the National Park Service viewpoint."[38]

The tourist season at the Lion Farm lasted from spring through autumn. According to oral sources, during the busy months, one thousand or more people might pass through the Lion Farm daily.[39] By the late 1940s, the signage at the Lion Farm had been scaled down from the large billboards that predominated during the early years. According to Leonora Tietjen Wilhelm, who comanaged the Lion Farm during the 1950s, "Everyone knew where we were."[40] Larry Burke, who appraised the Lion Farm in the mid-1950s, noted:

> The first good view of the Painted Desert which the West bound traveler sees is within the boundaries of [the Lion Farm]. Personal observation, corroborated by statements from local residents, is that a large majority of these West bound travelers stop on [the Lion Farm] to view the Desert.[41]

In 1951, an appraisal report noted that the Lion Farm "probably is doing the best tourist business in the entire area,"[42] and by 1956, the Lion Farm was outselling all of its competitors.[43]

Park Service Support of the Painted Desert Inn

Not all roadside businesses were treated in the same way by the Park Service at Petrified Forest. Upscale pretensions and cultural refinement were both valued and rewarded by Superintendent Smith and his staff, to the detriment of other less sophisticated operations. During the 1930s, the contempt displayed by Park Service leaders with regard to "hot dog stands," "shanties," and "shacks" such as the Lion Farm differed dramatically from the approach adopted toward another local tourist business called the

Figure 12. Aerial view of the Lion Farm looking north across Route 66, 1955. Courtesy of Leonora Tietjen Wilhelm.

Figure 13. The Painted
Desert Inn, looking
northwest, 1934. The
Painted Desert is located
on the right, to the east.
The architecture of
the building displayed
elements of the Prairie
Style and created an
effect that was markedly
more sophisticated
than the Lion Farm.
From H. D. Moulton,
"Petrified Forest
National Monument,
Arizona, Chas. J. Smith,
Superintendent, Official
Conduct and Related
Matters. Favorable
Report" (November 24,
1934); RG 79, Central
Classified Files 1933–49;
National Archives and
Records Administration,
College Park, Maryland.

Painted Desert Inn (Figure 13). Located about a mile north of the Lion Farm on an overlook above the Painted Desert, the hotel was operated by H. D. Lore.[44]

Lore began constructing the large two-story building in 1924, utilizing pieces of petrified wood for its walls; he publicized the structure as "the only house in the world built of petrified wood."[45] A photograph from the era shows the dining room tastefully furnished with wooden tables and chairs (Figure 14). A tabletop was laid out for a meal with attractive place settings, candlesticks, and a centerpiece. Navajo rugs in a variety of designs hung from a banister and covered the floors. Blocks of petrified wood in one wall provided what must have been an imposing background for an oversized rug that Lore advertised as "the largest 'Sand Painting' Navajo blanket in existence."[46] The photograph conveys an overall effect that is understated and elegant.[47] B. B. Craig, of the U.S. General Land Office, described the Painted Desert Inn as "beautiful" and "admired by thousands of people a year."[48] Superintendent Smith, for his part, was known

to have brought official guests to visit the Inn and tour the Painted Desert with Lore.[49]

The pleasing and tasteful quality of the Inn provided an added incentive for the Park Service to acquire the Painted Desert. Placing the area around Route 66 under Park Service jurisdiction also provided an ideal opportunity to gain control over other roadside businesses that were viewed with rather less favor.

In February 1932, Roger Toll, superintendent of Yellowstone National Park, was asked by the director of the National Park Service to travel to Arizona and evaluate the Painted Desert area as a possible addition to Petrified Forest National Monument. During both of his visits that month, Toll inspected the area with Superintendent Smith and H. D. Lore. Lore owned some 2,500 acres in the immediate area, most located on the mesa occupied by the Painted Desert Inn, and all eventually purchased by the Park Service. Toll felt that Lore's Rim Road, which followed the perimeter of the mesa, provided "the best view of the Painted Desert that can be obtained by automobiles."[50] Toll's report also indicates that

Figure 14. The dining room of the Painted Desert Inn with "the largest 'Sand Painting' Navajo blanket in existence" mounted on the rear wall, circa 1930. Courtesy of the Petrified Forest National Park Archives.

the architecture he saw as appropriate for the Painted Desert followed in the tradition of the grand hotels found in several western National Parks. Toll greatly admired the Painted Desert Inn and likened it to El Tovar (1905), the great lodge at Grand Canyon National Park.[51]

In March 1932, Horace Albright, director of the National Park Service, wrote Toll and enclosed a map indicating the areas he wanted to incorporate into the Painted Desert addition. Albright recommended that the new boundaries include a section on the eastern rim of the Painted Desert that included the Lion Farm. Albright justified his decision to expand the monument in this area, explaining:

> We came down to the highway in this stretch for we are under the impression that the highway comes right close to the rim in this township. It would also give us an opportunity to eventually do away with the lion farm which is located somewhere along this section of the road, overlooking the Painted Desert.[52]

For Albright, the mandate was clear: The Lion Farm would have to go, and with its demolition, a "natural landscape" would be established along the edge of the Painted Desert.

The federal government's effort to close the Lion Farm was halted by State Land Commissioner Howard J. Smith. Not everyone agreed with the Park Service that the Lion Farm was a blight on the landscape. In fact, Commissioner Smith wrote in 1932:

> Section 2, upon which is located the so-called Lions [sic] Farm, represents one of the most valuable and interesting scenic attractions found anywhere in the Southwest. Its value in dollar and cents is impossible of computation as it could not be duplicated. Its power, if properly developed, will be the magnet for attracting thousands of tourists and thousands of dollars.[53]

Negotiations to acquire Section 2 from the state of Arizona continued, but various complications, including the issue of providing compensation for the buildings and improvements constructed on the site would prevent the transfer of the land to the National Park Service for the next thirty years.

With the addition of the Painted Desert to the monument, plans were set in motion to provide federal funding to pave the Rim Road constructed by H. D. Lore. Not only did this road offer spectacular views of the Painted Desert; it also provided direct access to the Painted Desert Inn from Route 66.

H. D. Lore would not sell his hotel to the National Park Service until 1936. Nevertheless, a federal investigation in 1934 concluded that the Park Service openly favored the Painted Desert Inn over other local tourist-oriented businesses in the area. Lion Farm owner Julia Miller's role in collecting signatures and organizing local support was central to prompting the Department of the Interior to act on the situation. A petition sent to Secretary of the Interior Harold Ickes in September 1934 asked that the Painted Desert area be removed from Petrified Forest National Monument, calling it "a great and expensive attraction to enrich the few and to improverish [sic] the less opulent places of business carried on in this vicinity."[54] The petition was followed up by a letter from a local grievance committee, led by Miller, to President Franklin Roosevelt in October 1934, questioning why the Rim Road was being improved by the government, when "there is more than a mile of Highway 66 which now follows the rim of the Painted Desert, over which course of one mile, the traveler may view all of the beauties of the Painted Desert." The signers suggested that paving Lore's road would

> greatly enhance privately owned lands and place in the hands of the Park Service the power to direct traffic of the traveling public to the detriment and financial ruin of many of the pioneers of Arizona who have invested their life savings in small business enterprizes [sic] to entertain and direct tourists in viewing the Painted Desert and other beauties of Arizona.[55]

Superintendent Smith seems to have countered Julia Miller's charges by mounting his own attack. He complained to his superiors in Washington that the Lion Farm was "an unsightly, unsanitary place," adding, "We do not go out of our way to direct visitors to her place, it is true. In fact we simply ignore its existence since it is a place which would offend the sensibilities of any refined person."[56] Smith was particularly concerned about the zoo. He mentioned that the animals were fed on horsemeat and that sometimes "the stench from the inclosure is overpowering."[57] Smith felt that the monument was taking the only course of action possible with regard to the Lion Farm, noting that, "Should we direct tourists to this place, it would signify approval by the National Park Service of these penned up animals and other undesirable features."

In the midst of the fracas, Secretary Ickes offered his own appraisal of the Lion Farm, writing that, "While I have never gone into Mrs. Miller's place, I have passed it on a number of occasions and I have felt it to be a blot on the scenery."[58] Julia Miller nearly achieved all of her objectives when the Interior Department report recommended Superintendent Smith's transfer. Nevertheless, Smith retained his post at Petrified Forest and oversaw the continued development of Lore's property when it was bought, along with the Painted Desert Inn, by the National Park Service on February 29, 1936.

Reacting to Roadside Architecture with Parkitecture

In contrast to the commercial vernacular buildings of the Lion Farm, the Park Service at Petrified Forest came to favor two architectural idioms that also had commercial overtones. The Spanish–Pueblo Revival style adopted during the 1920s, 1930s, and 1940s has its roots in the late nineteenth century, when "pseudopueblos" were constructed by the railroads and other capitalist entities to publicize "the American Southwest" as a tourist destination at various world's fairs.[59] The International Style architecture constructed in succeeding years at Petrified Forest is markedly similar to contemporary shopping centers designed by Victor Gruen.

The Spanish–Pueblo Revival style attained its most profound expression in the city of Santa Fe, where it has been specifically employed to promote tourism. In the early twentieth century, civic leaders in Santa Fe including Jesse Nusbaum and Edgar Lee Hewett "repackaged" the community and in the process developed an iconic Southwestern architecture.[60] Their handiwork offered a vision of the region that was "untouched by modernity" and pared down to a set of easily digested motifs.[61] The architecture of Santa Fe helped to commodify the Southwest, and its characteristic style was selected by Park Service designers for Petrified Forest.

Between 1937 and 1940, the Park Service transformed the Painted Desert Inn into a landmark example of the Spanish–Pueblo Revival style (Figure 15).[62] The building was still formally linked to its setting, but now the connection was furnished by thickly plastered walls that mimicked the sensual, almost fleshy contours of the area's topography. The flat-roofed, parapeted exterior was covered with stucco rendered to appear like adobe in texture and color.[63] Park Service designer Lyle Bennett incorporated all of the hallmarks of the Spanish–Pueblo Revival style into the building, including *vigas*, thick wooden lintels, *zapatas* (carved corbels), *ramadas*, wooden grilles, *canales* (long, protruding scuppers), and *bancos* (built-in benches). The interior is embellished throughout with Native American design motifs, and custom-built furnishings include tinwork, light fixtures, and mirrors demonstrating a Spanish Colonial influence.[64] A public gas station, pumphouse, powerhouse, equipment building, and two residences were all constructed in a style to match the Inn and create a Spanish–Pueblo Revival "village."[65]

The Painted Desert Inn possesses several features that qualify it as an example of Park Service Rustic architecture. Its earthen-colored walls bear a similarity to the bentonite cliffs of the Painted Desert. The low-slung structure cleaves to the ground in a way that helps to blend it into its setting. Lorimer Skidmore, the supervising architect for the project, claimed that the Painted Desert Inn is "entirely in character being located in the heart of Hopi, Navajo, and Zuni Indian Country."[66] Nevertheless, historian William E. Brown has noted that the style of the building "is really not indigenous to this part of Arizona at all. The Rio Grande Valley [in central New Mexico] was the center of historic period Pueblo-Spanish architecture, upon which the revival is based." Brown added, however that "in a Southwest regional context, the building fits."[67]

In 1938, the Park Service constructed a new entrance station at the eastern junction of the Rim Road with Route 66. Like other Park Service

Figure 15. The Painted Desert Inn, looking east, circa 1940s. Courtesy of the Petrified Forest National Park Archives (catalog no. 20719).

Figure 16. The Park
Service Painted Desert
Checking Station, looking
north across Route 66,
1949. Courtesy of the
Petrified Forest National
Park Archives (catalog
no. 1568).

buildings in the Painted Desert, this structure
was executed in an imitation adobe, Spanish–
Pueblo Revival style (Figure 16). Apart from
the Inn, it was almost certainly the most elabo-
rately detailed example at the monument. The
structure, now demolished, had a wooden grille,
canal, thick wooden lintels, and *vigas.* A sloping,
buttressed wall recalled the Church of San Francisco at Ranchos de Taos, New Mexico, an iconic
example of Pueblo-influenced Spanish Colonial
architecture.[68] The new entrance station, located
immediately off Route 66, was entirely in keeping with the architecture of Santa Fe, Taos, and
the University of New Mexico, also located on
Route 66 in Albuquerque.[69]

The choice of the Spanish–Pueblo Revival
style for the entrance station and the Painted
Desert buildings (located a mile off of Route 66)
was hardly a coincidence. Petrified Forest is positioned approximately halfway between Santa Fe
and the Grand Canyon, the site of two of architect
Mary Jane Elizabeth Colter's Spanish–Pueblo
Revival masterpieces, Hopi House (1905), the
first Spanish–Pueblo Revival structure in the
National Park system, and Indian Watchtower at
Desert View (1932).[70] The Indian Watchtower was
constructed as a "mystical fantasy" and based on
the prehistoric architecture of Hopi pueblos and
Anasazi sites.[71]

In 1947, the concession at the Painted Desert
Inn was turned over to the Fred Harvey Company, and Colter was called in to complete her
last commission as an employee of the company
where she had spent the last forty-five years of
her career.[72] She changed the paint scheme and
added picture windows on the eastern Painted
Desert façade. Perhaps more important, however, Colter asked famed Hopi artist Fred Kabotie
to paint a series of murals for the Inn. Kabotie
had previously done work for Colter at the Indian
Watchtower, where he decorated the Hopi Room
with images based on Hopi life and ceremony.
The murals at the Painted Desert Inn show some
obvious similarities both in content and style
to the murals at the Indian Watchtower. The
remodeling done during 1947 and 1948 further
cemented the architectural connection between
the Grand Canyon and Petrified Forest.

It is surely significant that the designer of
Hopi House ended her career at a landmark
example of the style that she helped popularize.
Both Hopi House and the Painted Desert Inn are
related to each other by their architecture. They
are also both rooted in an ideology based on "Selling the Southwest."

Although the Fred Harvey Company and the
city planners of Santa Fe may have used Spanish–Pueblo Revival as a means to economic gain,

they were never aggressive about the commercial objectives underlying their choice of architectural expression. The style could entice people merely with its romantic overtones and aesthetic beauty. The Park Service was able to employ this "refined sensibility" by appropriating Spanish–Pueblo Revival architecture. The contrast between the subtlety of this approach and the kitschiness of contemporary commercial vernacular architecture is stark. Between 1938 and 1953, the Spanish–Pueblo Revival entrance station and the Lion Farm stood only a few hundred feet away from each other along Route 66 (Figure 17). It is tempting to conclude that the architectural detail lavished on the station was intended to draw people away from the Lion Farm. The juxtaposition must have been dramatic.

The 1940s and 1950s: Renewed Efforts to Control the Lion Farm

Complaints that the Lion Farm was an eyesore continued into the 1940s. Park Service officials worried that visitors to the monument would perceive that the roadside business was owned and operated by the federal government and would be seen as part of the Park Service entrance to Petrified Forest. A memorandum dated June 10, 1946 from Superintendent Thomas Whitcraft stated that the Lion Farm unquestionably "gives the

monument a bad reputation."[73] In August 1951, Superintendent William E. Branch reported:

The area has been cleaned up and is now presentable, but regardless of its condition, those of the several million people crossing the Monument on Highway 66 yearly, who stop at this place (Old Lion Farm), gain the impression it is operated by the Monument.[74]

The official name of the Lion Farm, "The Painted Desert Park," probably helped to divert tourists, but there was little that the Park Service could do. A similar situation prevailed at Carlsbad Caverns National Monument, where "a tourist court" had been given a title that incorporated the words "Carlsbad Caverns." In May 1953, the Chief Counsel for the Park Service stated that the Park Service had no legal recourse to the confusion that this may have created. Although the staff at Carlsbad Caverns could encourage the business to desist from implying that it was affiliated with the Park Service, the name was in itself perfectly legal.[75]

In the next decade, the Park Service tried another tactic to rid the landscape of the Lion Farm. This time, they attempted to cut the private establishment off from Route 66 and thus oust the Lion Farm from its position near the

Figure 17. The Park Service Painted Desert Checking Station, looking south from the parking lot of the Lion Farm, early 1950s. Courtesy of Leonora Tietjen Wilhelm.

monument. During the early 1950s, Route 66 was set to be relocated and in January 1954, the project map established that the Lion Farm was to be circumvented by six-tenths of a mile from the new alignment.[76] By the following May, the Park Service had decided to reroute the entrance road to the Painted Desert. In July, Acting Regional Director Hugh M. Miller stated his intention to use this strategy to leave the Lion Farm "high and dry" and force it off the Painted Desert rim.[77] By November 1955, a spur road connecting the Lion Farm to the new alignment of Route 66 had been completed (see Figure 2).[78] Although displaced from the main highway, the business continued to stay open.

In mid-1956, the president of Painted Desert Park, Inc., Albert Tietjen, offered to sell the Park Service the buildings and improvements associated with the business.[79] Tietjen and his business partner, federal Bureau of Indian Affairs Commissioner Glenn Emmons, offered a purchasing price of $125,000 for the Lion Farm in August of that year.[80] Earlier in the same month, Fagergren had fortuitously encountered two engineers from the Bureau of Public Roads and a discussion of the ramifications of the new Federal Aid Highway Act had ensued. According to Fagergren, one of the engineers stated that the Act "is very restrictive of access roads," adding that "he doubted if the presently approved spur road to the Lion Farm would be permitted."[81] Like his predecessors, Fagergren harbored little affection for the Lion Farm and looked forward to the time when it would be possible to "remove the unsightly structures on the rim" and "gain an 'exclusive' of the Painted Desert."[82]

By mid-October 1957, the Park Service had requested that the state obliterate the section of old Route 66 that remained within its boundaries; this action would cut off the east and west approaches to the Lion Farm. During the same month, plans were being laid to "block off" the spur road that connected the Lion Farm with the new alignment of Route 66.[83] The effect of this course of action would be to completely isolate the Lion Farm from its source of revenue. By July 1958, it appeared that this was not just an idle threat. Albert Tietjen, co-owner of the Lion Farm, was so concerned that the spur road would be closed that he asked his lawyer to write the State Land Commissioner, requesting that it remain open. In his letter, attorney Earl Platt noted that the Park Service was refusing to allow a sign "showing the existence of the Painted Desert Park."[84] Through careful planning, the government was well on its way to orchestrating the demise of the Lion Farm.

Meanwhile, the Park Service pursued efforts to buy the Lion Farm, offering $40,000 for the property in August 1957. As the federal government and the Lion Farm owners dickered over the price, the new interstate highway opened. Park Superintendent Fagergren specifically noted in his July 1958 monthly report that "this new road by-passes the old Lion Farm and the only views of the Painted Desert are now within the Monument."[85]

Mission 66: A New Phase of Park Service Architecture and Planning

By 1956, the Park Service was laying plans for a new development to be located about a mile west of the Lion Farm. The project was part of Mission 66, a massive nationwide program to rebuild and revitalize the infrastructure of the Park Service. Devised in 1955 by Park Service Director Conrad Wirth, Mission 66 was planned for a ten-year period and slated for completion in 1966, the fiftieth anniversary of the Park Service.[86]

Mission 66 introduced a number of important innovations to Park Service architecture. A new type of facility, the visitor center, was created to serve tourists. Park Service designers also embraced a new architectural style that presented a radical departure from the architecture that had dominated the Park Service from shortly after its inception.[87] The picturesque and rustic qualities that characterized earlier buildings disappeared, and the materials of mainstream Modernist architecture, particularly concrete, steel and glass, played a much larger role. Horizontality predominated—roofs tended to be flat, and building profiles clung to the ground.[88]

The Mission 66 architectural agenda shaped the new visitor center planned for the Painted Desert. Like other visitor centers, the new facility near the Painted Desert was to unite a variety of services into one building and include a restaurant, gas station, and a store. The result would be to provide a stress-free, "one-stop" experience for tourists traveling on the new Route 66 (soon to become I-40).[89]

The 1960 master plan for the Painted Desert visitor center also highlighted the fact that the new highway configuration prevented the presence of unwanted commercial landscapes around the Painted Desert. It noted:

the impetus to the Painted Desert Developments was provided by the construction of Interstate Highway No. 40 (US Highway 66) a controlled access highway replacing an older route which, being located near the rim, has fostered the growth of several unsightly commercial areas on adjoining land. The desert is no longer visible from the new highway location, and the only access to the rim is through the monument interchange.[90]

Park Service architects identified a site and drew up a set of initial plans, and by 1958, the government had engaged the firm of Richard Neutra and Robert Alexander to complete the visitor center.[91] This was the second Park Service commission for Neutra and Alexander. Earlier in the same year, they had also been hired to design the

Visitor Center and Cyclorama Building at Gettysburg National Military Park.[92]

The new visitor center at Petrified Forest, known as the Painted Desert Community (1958–1965), was originally composed of gleaming white surfaces, broad expanses of glass, and uninterrupted planes of brick and stone (Figure 18). The simple lines, horizontal profile and dark gray brick of the complex helped it blend into the rolling grasslands that surround it. Its exterior walls presented a homogeneous façade with expanses of unfenestrated masonry that served to make the buildings even more unassuming (Figure 19). The overall effect was neat, contained, and bland. Visitors would arrive at the complex to find long, unadorned walls that channeled pedestrians into a plaza surrounded by the visitor center, gift shop, and restaurant.[93] The complex still incorporates a broad array of facilities; all the buildings are combined into one overarching design and united by a common architectural style.

The original plan of the Painted Desert Community maintained a strict sense of separation between automobiles and pedestrians.[94] The gas station is located at some remove from the rest of the buildings, and two landscaped islands in the

Figure 18. The plaza of the Painted Desert Community, looking west, 1963. The plaza is surrounded by a restaurant, a gift shop, a visitor center, administrative offices, a large community room/auditorium, and a small post office. Photograph by August Beinlich. Courtesy of the Petrified Forest National Park Archives (catalog no. 1762-16).

Figure 19. The Painted Desert Community, viewed from the north, with architect Richard Neutra pictured on the right, 1963. Photograph by August Beinlich. Courtesy of the Petrified Forest National Park Archives (catalog no. 1762-15).

parking lot provide a further barrier. It is difficult not to contrast this layout with the way that Route 66 architecture catered to the automobile. Parking lots lined the road, and building entrances were located only a few steps away.

Although the Painted Desert Community bore the distinguishing marks of a Richard Neutra design, the architects made a limited attempt to relate the main visitor area to the surrounding regional context. Two elements evocative of Southwest architecture were incorporated into the plan. The first was the layout of the visitor area, which was arranged around a plaza enclosed on three sides.[95] Neutra described this feature as related to Anasazi ruins and Spanish Colonial architecture.[96] Neutra also designed the south wall of the plaza with a masonry veneer, to be executed with "a crude Indian workmanship somewhat similar to what the Indians have used in this area for so many hundreds of years."[97] Although inspired by historic architecture, the plaza and wall were readily subsumed into the predominant International Style of the project.

The Painted Desert Community bears a striking resemblance to contemporary shopping centers designed by Victor Gruen.[98] In an ironic twist, the Park Service chose to construct an example

of cutting-edge commercial architecture, while viewing a representative of the commercial vernacular with unrelieved disapproval. Gruen's designs were profit-oriented ventures, to be sure, but they also organized disparate elements into one overarching plan and provided areas for people to rest and socialize—these qualities were also considered desirable for Park Service visitor centers. Neutra almost certainly did not intend his scheme to resemble a shopping center; however, with the addition of a landscape plan designed by Neutra and Park Service architects, the complex came to bear a pronounced likeness to some of Gruen's most famous designs. This parallelism may be due to the fact that Neutra and Gruen had similar backgrounds—both architects grew up and trained in Vienna and counted Adolf Loos as a primary influence.[99]

In building I-40 and the Painted Desert Community, the federal government endorsed a new approach to handling travelers that prized efficiency. The interstate highway system made it possible to journey long distances without interruption. Wayside businesses were relegated to frontage roads, and the close relationship that once existed between the highway and the communities it passed through was sacrificed for the sake of optimizing speed. The new visitor center can be seen as an extension of Interstate 40. The highway, which streamlined travel through the area beginning in 1958, channels traffic directly into the Painted Desert Community with a dedicated off-ramp. There are no entrance stations to obstruct the few hundred yards that lie between the cloverleaf and the buildings. The connection between the highway and the visitor center is seamless.

Late Developments

The Park Service was able to capitalize on the location of the new interstate to sever the Lion Farm from its customers. For years, Park Service leaders had been working to remove the roadside business from the rim of the Painted Desert, through means both legal and not. Then, through the introduction of the highways system, access ramps, and visitors' center the goal was achieved almost effortlessly. The only off-ramp in the area led directly into the Painted Desert Community, and the only views of the Painted Desert were accessible after passing through a Park Service entrance station. The appearance of the Painted Desert landscape was now entirely under the purview of the Park Service.

In 1960, the rental agreement for Section 2 was up for renewal with the State of Arizona. For nearly two years, the Lion Farm had been cut off from any kind of access that would have yielded income. The owner, Albert Tietjen, attempted to extend his contract, but his plans were subverted by Park Service officials, who had been working with the Arizona State Land Office to outmaneuver him.

By June 23, 1960, Arizona State Land Commissioner Obed Lassen had terminated the lease. Tietjen had previously given Lassen a list of improvements associated with the Lion Farm worth an estimated $48,000.[100] Tietjen then filed an appeal with the Superior Court in Apache County, and on July 10, 1961, arguments began in *Painted Desert Park, Inc. v. State Land Department.*

Tietjen may have tried to renew the lease as a way to ensure that the full value of the Lion Farm would be compensated. As long as he held control over the section, he would have some bargaining power. For the Park Service, finding the money to buy the improvements had been an obstacle back in the 1930s, and twenty-five years later, the same issue hindered efforts to finalize transfer of the land. By February 1960, a serious attempt had been made in Congress to allocate $100,000 to Petrified Forest for the purchase of nonfederal property within the monument, some of which would probably have been used to compensate Tietjen.[101] Apparently the high dollar figure was interpreted to mean that landowners were being overpaid, and lawmakers deleted the earmarked amount from the Interior Department budget.[102]

By September 1962, condemnation papers had been filed on Section 2.[103] In November, Superintendent Fagergren met with the local manager of the Arizona Public Service Company "to discuss their removal of power lines serving the 'Lion Farm' property."[104] The following month, U.S. Marshals were in the area looking for Leonora Tietjen Wilhelm, the manager of the Lion Farm.[105]

The transfer of Section 2 did not become final until September 9, 1970, when the Arizona State Land Department received a check for $50,000 from the federal government.[106] After paying Tietjen $48,000 for the improvements at the Lion Farm, the state ended up receiving only $2,000 for the property once described as "the most valuable section of land owned by the State in Arizona."[107]

Conclusion

Although developments like the Lion Farm were welcomed by many travelers, the Park Service aspired to protect the "natural" landscape of the Painted Desert. In 1957, as the Lion Farm prepared to close, J. B. Jackson published an essay extolling roadside architecture as "a kind of folk art," writing:

> I keep remembering the times I have driven for hour after hour across an emptiness—desert or prairie—which was *not* blemished by highway stands, and how relieved and delighted I always was to finally see somewhere in the distance the jumble of billboards and gas pumps and jerry-built houses. Tourist traps or not these were very welcome sights, and even the commands EAT, COME

AS YOU ARE, GAS UP, GET FREE ICE WATER AND STICKERS, had a comforting effect.[108]

But, ultimately, the Park Service officials who guided Petrified Forest through the 1930s, 1940s, and 1950s endeavored to remove the Lion Farm and other "undesirable developments," and establish their own architectural vision of the area. The Spanish–Pueblo Revival buildings erected between 1929 and 1942 tied the monument to other areas of the Southwest. They "themed" Petrified Forest, and gave it an air of premodernity and fantasy. In fact, it is probably fair to characterize these buildings as belonging to a distinctly American type of architectural folly.

With the Painted Desert Community, the Park Service opted for a dramatic contrast to the Painted Desert Inn. Whether Neutra's design had a commercial provenance is debatable; what is clear is that the new visitor center presented a modern, "up-to-date" appearance and a typology that would have been familiar to many visitors during the early 1960s. Documents indicate that the structure was intended to serve as a flagship for other national parks and monuments in the region. As a consequence, the image it presented was important, but in keeping with the overall Mission 66 ideology, the visitor center also placed a premium on functionality. The Painted Desert Community channeled movement so that travelers would find their sojourn to be free of confusion and stress. The excitement and risk inherent in stopping at an independent "Mom and Pop" Route 66 roadside establishment were abandoned in favor of efficiency and predictability.

Now that the rim of the Painted Desert is free from the Lion Farm, visitors can enjoy the sublime power of unobstructed nature. Alternatively, they can fully absorb the atmosphere of an imitation pueblo where, to this day, Native American artisans are hired to demonstrate their skills. Or perhaps historian Hal Rothman is correct when he asserts that an American sense of identity relies on understanding the natural wonders of the West as equivalent to the European cultural landscape.[109] The Painted Desert, a landscape that is "sacred" to the American mythos, has

now been stripped of "profane" elements like the Lion Farm and placed at a remove from I-40. The dedicated off-ramp, park drive, and entrance station reflect the processional quality of approach sequences found in many examples of religious architecture. The area has an almost apocalyptic quality created by its barrenness, strange colors, and setting in a concave depression that bears resemblance to a crater. The familiarity of a commercial vernacular structure on its rim would go far to diminish the sense of mystery and privation that underlies its appeal.

The location of the old Lion Farm now lies on a service road that is off-limits to visitors. Clearly, for the Park Service, the value of Section 2 was not in the vistas that extend from its site. The reason for "doing away" with the Lion Farm was to arrange an unobstructed view of the Painted Desert. "Unobstructed" is perhaps the wrong word. After all, the Lion Farm never prevented anyone on the Rim Road from seeing the Painted Desert. What the Lion Farm did do was interject an example of the American vernacular landscape that interfered with the experience that the Park Service was seeking to create.

The demolition of the Lion Farm was part of a larger movement to efface certain types of cultural landscapes in and around national parks and monuments. Many of these attempts were unsuccessful due to various political forces that circumscribed the degree to which the federal government could control activity outside Park Service boundaries.[110] The Lion Farm, however, was located squarely within the boundaries of Petrified Forest, and when the opportunity arose, the Park Service was able to control access and work with the State of Arizona to bring about its demise.

While the empty expanses of the park perpetuate one type of American myth, Route 66 and the Lion Farm now embody another (Figure 20). The "eyesore" that once stood on the edge of the Painted Desert epitomized a distinctive variety of Route 66 travel culture that paradoxically, is now viewed with nostalgia. Nearly fifty years have passed since the Lion Farm was obliterated from the landscape of the Painted Desert. The Park Service officials who brought about its closing

could never have envisioned the romance that would come to be associated with old Route 66 and its "honky-tonk improvisations," sites exemplified by the Lion Farm.[111]

NOTES
The author would like to thank Charles J. Jacobs, Bill Miller, Elda Tietjen Powell, Jo Rhodes, Gloria Olsen Slipher, and Leonora Tietjen Wilhelm for their generosity and willingness to provide photographs and oral historical material about the Lion Farm. The archival assistance of Scott Williams of the National Park Service has been invaluable to the development of this article. I would also like to thank Daniel Bluestone, Marta Gutman, Louis Nelson, John R. Stein, Marianne Werner, Richard Guy Wilson, and the anonymous reader selected by *Buildings & Landscapes* for their helpful suggestions and comments.

1. "Presidential Proclamation No. 697," December 8, 1906. The Antiquities Act authorized the President of the United States to reserve federal lands for the purpose of protecting historic and natural resources. Three other monuments were also designated in 1906: Devil's Tower (September 24, 1906), El Morro (December 8, 1906), and Montezuma Castle (December 8, 1906). Petrified Forest became a national park on December 8, 1962.

2. The first Park Service building within Petrified Forest was a small, wood-clad museum. In "Letter from the Custodian, Petrified Forest National Monument to the Director, NPS," September 8, 1921,

Figure 20. Looking east from the Lion Farm along Route 66, early 1950s. Courtesy of Leonora Tietjen Wilhelm.

William Nelson declared, "the cabin [museum] has been built." Later correspondence ("Letter from Wm. Nelson, Custodian, Petrified Forest National Monument to the Director, NPS," April 27, 1924) indicates that the dimensions of the museum were 16 x 16 feet. In "Letter from Arno B. Cammerer, Acting Director, NPS to Wm. P. Nelson, Custodian, Petrified Forest National Monument," Cammerer enjoined, "You should paint the cabin green with white trimmings to match the National Park Service colors, green and white." All documents located in Petrified Forest National Park Archives [PFNP hereafter]. A photograph of the museum dating from July 16, 1929, may be found in the PFNP Archives (Catalog no. 20820).

3. The term "flamboyant hucksterism" is from Chester Liebs in *Main Street to Miracle Mile: American Roadside Architecture*, 2nd ed. (Baltimore: The Johns Hopkins Press, 1995), 20.

4. Petrified wood may be found in large concentrations (or "forests") throughout an area extending from western New Mexico to central Arizona.

5. Charles Lummis, "Stone Trees—A Forest Gone to Bed," *Santa Fe Employee's Magazine* 6, no. 7 (June 1912): 32.

6. The business was originally known as the "Desert View Station" but was renamed "Painted Desert Park and Mountain Lion Farm" around 1930. Shortly after 1940, the zoo was removed, and the official name became "Painted Desert Park." Government documents from the 1930s onward refer to the establishment as "The Lion Farm," and for the sake of consistency, that is the name that will be used here.

7. Telephone conversation with Charles J. Jacobs, August 12, 2008. Thomas Repp's *Route 66: The Romance of the West* (Lynnwood, Wash.: Mock Turtle Press, 2002) contains a detailed social history of the Lion Farm dating from its construction through circa 1950. Harry E. Miller figures prominently in this book, and a photo of him dominates the front cover. His older sister Julia Miller had four children—William, Charles H., Paul, and Joseille—all of whom worked at the Lion Farm at one time or another. Paul Jacobs's wife (Charles J. Jacobs's mother) Betty Jacobs, a Navajo woman, also worked at the store. Harry E. Miller was involved with at least three roadside businesses along Route 66, including Fort Two Guns and the Cave of the Seven Devils. All three of Miller's Route 66 ventures included a zoo. Miller may also have been one of the first persons to erect billboards along Route 66. See

Repp, *Route 66*, 161.

8. According to oral histories, Desert View Station was originally located on the south side of Route 66. By the early 1930s, the business had been moved to the north side of the highway, adjacent to the rim of the Painted Desert.

9. According to Daniel Bluestone in "Roadside Blight and the Reform of Commercial Architecture," there were 59,000 roadside stands in operation in 1929. See this essay in *Roadside America: The Automobile in Design and Culture*, ed. Jan Jennings (Ames: Iowa State University Press for the Society for Commercial Archeology, 1990), 178.

10. Bluestone, "Roadside Blight and the Reform of Commercial Architecture," 176.

11. Liebs, *Main Street to Miracle Mile*, 44.

12. Ibid., 43.

13. According to Gloria Olsen Slipher, who grew up at Overpass Curio, another roadside business located within Petrified Forest. Conversation, November 26, 2006.

14. As indicated by company letterhead on "Letter from Julia Miller to B. B. Moeur, Governor of Arizona," December 3, 1934. Arizona State Land Department Archives, Phoenix, Arizona.

15. Among film critics, there is a general consensus that Humphrey Bogart's breakout role was as "the heavy" in the movie *Petrified Forest* (1936), also starring Bette Davis and Leslie Howard. The action takes place within a diner located in a barren, desert area. A neon sign advertising BBQ sandwiches adorns the outside of the establishment. Although the Lion Farm did not physically resemble the building in the film, it is probable that it served as its inspiration.

16. Conversation with Slipher, November 26, 2006.

17. Marguerite Shaffer, *See America First: Tourism and National Identity* (Washington DC: Smithsonian Institution Press, 2001), 62.

18. Superintendent Charles Smith, "Report on Complaint of Mrs. Julia G. Miller," August 5, 1933, 4–5. NARA—College Park, Maryland, RG 79, Central Classified Files, 1933–1949.

19. Conversation with Jo Rhodes, September 9, 2006.

20. Ibid. Car doors built before the mid-1930s were wood-framed with relatively flat panels of sheet metal, making them well suited to serve as roofing material.

21. Liebs, *Main Street to Miracle Mile*, 50–51.

22. See, for example, letters and reports at the Petrified Forest National Park Archives, "File for Section 2, T 19N, R 24E" at the archives of the Arizona State Land Department, Phoenix, "Transcript of Proceedings—*Painted Desert Park, Inc. v. State Land Department*, Case nos. 3603 and 3661," Courthouse, St. John's Arizona, July 10, 1961, in the files of the Clerk of the Court, Apache County, St. John's Arizona, and documents located in RG 79, Central Classified Files, 1933–1949 at NARA—College Park, Maryland and in RG 79, Southwest Regional Office, Santa Fe at NARA—Rocky Mountain Region, Denver.

23. Ibid., 20.

24. Bluestone, "Roadside Blight and the Reform of Commercial Architecture," 172.

25. Ibid.

26. "Letter from B. B. Craig to The Commissioner, General Land Office," May 7, 1931. Part of "The Toll Report." PFNP Archives.

27. "Letter from Charles J. Smith, Superintendent to The Director of the National Park Service," June 8, 1931. PFNP Archives. In a report filed on August 5, 1933, Smith claimed that the Lion Farm had "a large sign reading Petrified Forest" when he first arrived at the Monument in August 1929. It seems likely that Smith's comments on June 8, 1931, were directed at the Lion Farm. See Smith, "Report on Complaint of Mrs. Julia G. Miller."

28. Hal Rothman, *Devil's Bargains: Tourism in the Twentieth-Century American West* (Lawrence: University of Kansas Press, 1998), 54.

29. Testimony of J. Leslie Hansen in the Superior Court of the State of Arizona in and for the County of Apache, "Transcript of Proceedings—*Painted Desert Park, Inc. v. State Land Department*, Case nos. 3603 and 3661," Courthouse, St. John's Arizona, July 10, 1961, 199–200. Clerk of the Court, Apache County, St. John's Arizona.

30. According to Repp in *Route 66* (130), the sale took the form of a real estate trade, in which Miller swapped the Lion Farm for a sanitarium owned by her daughter Joseille, who then swapped the Lion Farm for the Navajo Indian Village, a Route 66 business owned by Joseille's brother Charles H. Jacobs.

31. According to official records, Charles H. Jacobs, Albert Tietjen (jointly listed as "Tietjen-Jacobs"), and a third party named "Brentaria" leased the section on February 27, 1941. According to Slipher (conversation November 26, 2006), there were five individuals in the original partnership, including her step-grandfather, Willis Lynch. The lease was then renewed in 1945 by "Painted Desert Park, Inc.," under the names of "Tietjen-Jacobs" and "Emmons." "Emmons" referred to Glenn L. Emmons, a Gallup banker who served as the Commissioner of Indian Affairs during the Eisenhower administration. In 1950, the lease was renewed again by "Painted Desert Park, Inc." This time Albert Tietjen is listed as the sole lessee and president. See "File for Section 2, T 19N, R 24E," located at the Arizona State Land Department Archives, Phoenix, Arizona.

32. "Superintendent's Report for April 1941," May 10, 1941. PFNP Archives.

33. Conversation with Leonora Tietjen Wilhelm and Elda Tietjen Powell, September 19, 2006.

34. For discussion of the architecture of the *hooghan nímazí* and the *chaha'oh,* see Stephen C. Jett and Virginia E. Spencer, *Navajo Architecture: Forms and Distributions* (Tucson: University of Arizona Press, 1981).

35. The Navajo Indian Village was located near Chambers, Arizona, and during the mid-1950s, the Painted Desert Tower was located near the present site of the Painted Desert visitor center within Petrified Forest National Park.

36. Conversation with Powell and Wilhelm, September 19, 2006.

37. See "Superintendent's Report for October 1950," November 13, 1950; "Superintendent's Report for February 1951," March 8, 1951; "Superintendent's Report for March 1951," April 11, 1951; "Superintendent's Report for April 1951," May 11, 1951; "Superintendent's Report for May 1951," June 13, 1951; "Superintendent's Report for June 1951," July 11, 1951; "Superintendent's Report for July 1951," August 8, 1951; "Superintendent's Report for August 1951," September 13, 1951; "Superintendent's Report for September," October 11, 1951. PFNP Archives.

38. John Kell, "Boundary Study Report, Petrified Forest National Park," June 1954. PFNP Archives.

39. Conversation with Powell and Wilhelm, September 19, 2006.

40. Ibid.

41. Larry Burke, "Appraisal of Sec. 2, T19N, R24E, G&SRB&M for the United States of America," December 14, 1956. PFNP Archives.

42. H. B. Embach, "Appraisal Report, All of Section 10, Twp 19N, R 24 E S $\frac{1}{2}$ S $\frac{1}{2}$; NE $\frac{1}{4}$ SE $\frac{1}{4}$; E $\frac{1}{2}$ NE $\frac{1}{4}$ Sec. 26, T 20 N, R 24 E. Apache County, Arizona

and within Petrified Forest National Monument," July 5, 1951. PFNP Archives.

43. Frank Kelly, "Appraisal Report for United States Department of the Interior National Park Service," August 15, 1957. PFNP Archives.

44. H. D. Lore also referred to his business as the Stone Tree House. The National Park Service, however, extensively remodeled the building in the Spanish–Pueblo Revival style beginning in 1937, after which point it was always referred to as the Painted Desert Inn.

45. "Painted Desert Inn" [pamphlet], circa 1931–32. Northern Arizona University Cline Library Digital Archives, Item no. 35688.

46. Ibid.

47. The upscale aspirations of H. D. Lore are indicated by news reported in the *Gallup Independent* [New Mexico] on September 14, 1928. An article entitled "Painted Desert to Get Big New Hotel" claims that Lore had engaged the services of Fitzhugh and Byron, a noted architectural firm from Phoenix, to design a $150,000 hotel near the site of the Painted Desert Inn. According to the National Register nomination for Fitzhugh and Byron's First Baptist Church, located at 302 West Monroe in Phoenix, "Lee M. Fitzhugh was one of Phoenix's foremost architects for 30 years." The new structure was to include forty guest rooms as well as a lounge, dining rooms, lobby, and curio room. Construction was to be of "native volcanic stone," while petrified wood from the Black Forest would be used to ornament some of the public areas. The old Painted Desert Inn was to be transformed into a museum. Although the article states that work was to commence on November 1, 1928, I have found no record that the new hotel ever progressed past the planning stages. At least three structures, by Fitzhugh and Byron, are on the National Register. Nomination forms for these buildings may be found in the files of the Arizona State Historic Preservation Office in Phoenix.

48. "Letter from B. B. Craig to The Commissioner, General Land Office," May 7, 1931. Part of "The Toll Report." PFNP Archives.

49. "Superintendent's Report for February 1931," March 5, 1931. PFNP Archives.

50. Roger Toll, "Report to the Director of the Park Service," March 21, 1932. PFNP Archives.

51. "Letter from Roger Toll to The Director of the National Park Service," March 14, 1932. PFNP Archives.

52. "Letter from Horace Albright to Roger Toll," March 11, 1932. PFNP Archives.

53. "Letter from Howard J. Smith, Land Commissioner, State of Arizona to Mr. Charles J. Smith, Superintendent, Petrified Forest National Monument," October 31, 1932. Arizona State Land Department Archives, Phoenix, Arizona.

54. See "Petition to Honorable Harold L. Ickes, Secretary of the Interior," September 24, 1934. NARA—College Park, Maryland, RG 79, Central Classified Files, 1933–1949.

55. "Letter from George W. Payne, Julia G. Miller, Joseille Claude, Nora Lee Rice, [unreadable] Osborne, and [unreadable], Grievance Committee to Honorable Franklin D. Roosevelt, President of the United States," October 24, 1934. NARA—College Park, Maryland, RG 79, Central Classified Files, 1933–1949.

56. Chas. J. Smith, Superintendent, Petrified Forest National Monument, "Report on Complaint of Mrs. Julia G. Miller," August 5, 1933, 4. NARA—College Park, Maryland, RG 79, Central Classified Files, 1933–1949.

57. Ibid.

58. Harold L. Ickes, "Memorandum for Mr. Cammerer," August 19, 1933. NARA—College Park, Maryland, RG 79, Central Classified Files, 1933–1949.

59. Chris Wilson, *The Myth of Santa Fe* (Albuquerque: University of New Mexico Press, 1997), 115.

60. Rothman, *Devil's Bargains*, 81, 90–93.

61. Ibid., 94.

62. For example, *What Style Is It?* by John Poppeliers and S. Allen Chambers Jr. (Hoboken, N.J.: John Wiley, 2003), 24, offers the Painted Desert Inn as the representative example of the Pueblo Revival style.

63. Dewey Livingston et al., *Historic Structure Report: Painted Desert Inn, Petrified Forest National Park, Arizona*, (Denver, Colo.: National Park Service, October 1994), 58–59.

64. See Laura DeNormandie, *Historic Furnishings Report: Painted Desert Inn, Petrified Forest National Park* (Woods Hole, Mass.: Northeast Museum Services Center, National Park Service, 2004). Blueprints can be found in Department of Interior, National Park Service, Branch of Plans and Design, "Alterations and Additions to Lodge at Painted Desert, Petrified Forest National Monument," drawn January 15, 1937, revised March 31, 1937 (signed by Thomas Vint, Charles Smith and A. E. Demaray), available online at http://www.etic.Park Service.gov for registered users.

65. For more detail, see Lillian Makeda, "The Lion Farm and the National Park Service: Defining an Architectural Vision for Petrified Forest," MA thesis, University of Virginia, November 2006, chapter 2 ("Spanish–Pueblo Revival Architecture at Petrified Forest").

66. Lorimer Skidmore, "Report to the Chief of Planning on Construction of the Painted Desert Inn at Petrified Forest National Monument, Holbrook, Arizona," quoted in Laura Soullière Harrison, *Architecture in the Parks: National Historic Landmark Theme Study* (Washington D.C.: National Park Service, Department of the Interior, 1986), 446.

67. William E. Brown, "Summary Field Evaluation: Painted Desert Inn and Adjacent Residences," November 21, 1972, quoted in Livingston et al., *Historic Structure Report*, 45.

68. Ranchos de Taos is located northeast of Santa Fe and a few miles southwest of Taos. John Gaw Meem had already appropriated the buttresses on the church at Ranchos de Taos for his design of the Laboratory of Anthropology (1929) in Santa Fe. See Wilson, *Myth of Santa Fe*, 279.

69. This connection was made by Chris Wilson. Conversation, November 20, 2006.

70. Colter was employed by the Fred Harvey Company as an architect and interior designer beginning in 1903. Her work at Grand Canyon National Park, at the 1915 Panama-Pacific Exhibition in San Diego, and on railroad hotels including the Alvarado in Albuquerque; El Navajo in Gallup, New Mexico; and La Posada in Winslow, Arizona, was profoundly influential on perceptions of "the Southwest" as a cultural phenomenon.

71. Harrison's National Historic Landmark nomination, "M. E. J. Colter Buildings, Grand Canyon National Park," is reprinted in her book *Architecture in the Parks: National Historic Landmark Theme Study*, 109.

72. Virginia Grattan, *Mary Colter: Builder upon the Red Earth* (Grand Canyon, Ariz.: Grand Canyon Natural History Association, 1992), 102.

73. Thomas Whitcraft, "Memorandum for the Regional Director, Region III," ("A") June 10, 1946. NARA—Rocky Mountain Region Denver, RG 79, Southwest Regional Office, Santa Fe. Whitcraft sent two memorandums to the Regional Director on June 10, 1946, that I've designated as "A" and "B."

74. "Superintendent's Report for July 1951," August 8, 1951. PFNP Archives.

75. Chief Counsel, the NPS, "Memorandum to the Director," May 29, 1953. NARA—Rocky Mountain Region, Denver, RG 79, Southwest Regional Office, Santa Fe, New Mexico, Subject Correspondence Files, 1953–61.

76. "Superintendent's Report for January 1954," February 10, 1954. PFNP Archives.

77. Hugh M. Miller, Acting Regional Director, "Memorandum to Director," July 7, 1955. NARA—Rocky Mountain Region, Denver, RG 79, Southwest Regional Office, Santa Fe, New Mexico, Acquisition of Land Policy and Procedures, General Correspondence Files, May 1953–1961.

78. "Superintendent's Report for October 1955," November 12, 1955. PFNP Archives.

79. Hugh M. Miller, Regional Director, "Memorandum to Regional Chief of Operations," [stamped "Aug 1 1956"]. NARA—Rocky Mountain Region, Denver, RG 79, Southwest Regional Office, Santa Fe, New Mexico, Acquisition of Land Policy and Procedures, General Correspondence Files, May 1953–1961. Albert Tietjen was the son of a Mormon bishop with three wives. After a brief stint with the railroad ended, he began a career as a successful Indian trader, owning several posts, most notably Rocky Point Trading Post, located twelve miles west of Gallup on Route 66.

80. Information about these negotiations can be found in Fagergren's handwritten notes located in section L1425, PFNP Archives. Emmons was the President of the First State Bank of Gallup and knew Albert Tietjen because Tietjen sat on the Board of Directors of his bank. Emmons was the Republican nominee during the 1944 New Mexico gubernatorial campaign and held several national-level offices in the American Banking Association. He met Dwight Eisenhower at the Gallup Intertribal Ceremonial during Eisenhower's campaign for president in 1952 and subsequently served as federal Commissioner for the Bureau of Indian Affairs from 1953 to 1961. A copy of the June 1953 financial statement for the Painted Desert Park (as the Lion Farm was formally known) may be found in Box 1, Folder 4 of the Glenn Emmons Papers located at the Center for Southwest Research at the University of New Mexico, Albuquerque.

81. Fred Fagergren, Superintendent, "Memorandum to Regional Director, Region Three," August 3, 1956. NARA—Rocky Mountain Region, Denver, RG

79, Southwest Regional Office, Santa Fe, New Mexico, Acquisition of Land Policy & Procedures, General Correspondence Files, May 1953–1961.

82. Ibid.

83. Fred C. Fagergren, Superintendent, "Memorandum to Regional Director, Region Three," October 14, 1957. NARA—Rocky Mountain Region, Denver, RG 79, Southwest Regional Office, Santa Fe, New Mexico, Acquisition of Land Policy & Procedures, General Correspondence Files, May 1953–1961.

84. "Letter from Earl Platt to Mr. O. M. Lassen, State Land Commissioner," July 15, 1958. File for Case No. 3603/3661, *Painted Desert Park, Inc. v. State Land Department,* July 10, 1961. Clerk of the Superior Court, Apache County, St. John's, Arizona.

85. "Superintendent's Report for July 1958," August 13, 1958. PFNP Archives.

86. Ethan Carr, *Mission 66: Modernism and the National Park Dilemma* (Amherst, Mass.: University of Amherst Press, 2007), 64–65.

87. In 1918, Stephen Mather, the first director of the Park Service, put out a "Statement of Policy" that laid the foundation for what has been labeled as the Park Service rustic style. According to Mather, "In the construction of roads, trails, buildings, and other improvements, particular attention must be devoted always to the harmonizing of these improvements with the landscape."

88. Sarah Allaback, *Mission 66 Visitor Centers: The History of a Building Type* (Washington D.C.: U.S. Department of the Interior, 2000), 23. "The Mission 66 Visitor Centers, 1956–1966: Early Modern Architecture in the National Park Service" by Christine Madrid French (MA thesis, University of Virginia, 1998) also provides important background on the Mission 66 visitor centers.

89. "Mission 66 for Petrified Forest National Monument" (National Park Service, U.S. Department of the Interior, 1956), introduction, 6. PFNP Archives.

90. Weiler and Scheffler, "Master Plan for the Preservation and Use of Petrified Forest National Monument, Arizona," chapter 5, page 2.

91. Amanda Zeman, "Painted Desert Community Complex Historic District," National Register Nomination, April 15, 2005, section 8, pages 11–12.

92. Information about the ongoing battle to save the Cyclorama building from demolition may be found at http://www.mission66.com/cyclorama.

93. John Milner Associates in association with Woolpert, LLP, *Painted Desert Community Complex Historic District Cultural Landscape Report* (U.S. Department of the Interior, National Park Service, November 2005), chapter 2, page 10.

94. The separation has been diminished by the addition of a set of doors to the gift shop that open out into the parking lot.

95. Neutra and Alexander, Architects, "Painted Desert Visitor's Center, Arizona National Park Service, from conversations of Richard Neutra with Mr. Sanford Hill, Western Division National Park Service, Mr. Fagergren, Supt. Painted Desert, and Dr. Phil Van Cleave, Naturalist and Head of Interpretation Service," [n.d.], 2. PFNP Archives.

96. "Letter from Richard Neutra to Stewart Udall," April 13, 1961. PFNP Archives. Stewart Udall, secretary of the interior from 1961 through 1969, was born in St. John's, Arizona, located forty miles southeast of Petrified Forest. In 1957, he was a congressman, and according to a phone interview with Mr. Udall on November 20, 2006, he was not involved in the selection of Neutra for the Painted Desert Community. Udall wrote an article praising the Painted Desert Community titled "Can Federal Architecture Be Creative?" for *Arizona Architect* 6 (February 1963): 12–19.

97. "Interoffice Memorandum from R. J. N. to R. E. A. and J. C. R.," August 5, 1961. PFNP Archives.

98. According to Sarah Allaback, Neutra urged the Park Service to keep a blank façade along the parking lot because he felt that windows would have created the impression of a shopping center. See *Mission 66 Visitor Centers: The History of a Building Type,* chapter IV. Accessed online at http://www.nps.gov/history/history/online_books/allaback, July 27, 2009.

99. The two men were separated by eleven years: Neutra was born in 1892 and Gruen in 1903. Regarding Loos's influence, see Alex Wall, *Victor Gruen: From Urban Shop to New City* (Barcelona: Actar, 2005), 21; Thomas S Hines, *Richard Neutra and the Search for Modern Architecture* (Berkeley and Los Angeles: University of California Press, 1994), 18.

100. See "Findings of Fact, Case No. 3603/3661, *Painted Desert Park, Inc. v. State Land Department,* July 10, 1961. Courthouse, St. John's, AZ," and "File for Section 2, T 19N, R 24E." Both are located at the Arizona State Land Department Archives, Phoenix, Arizona.

101. See Fred C. Fagergren, "Memorandum to Director [of the Park Service], February 19, 1960; also see "Letter from Don T. Udall to Senator Carl Hayden," February 19, 1960. NARA—Rocky Mountain Region, Denver, RG 79, Southwest Regional Office, Santa Fe, New Mexico, Acquisition of Land Policy & Procedures, General Correspondence Files, May 1953–1961.

102. Ibid.

103. See papers regarding UNITED STATES OF AMERICA v. 637.80 ACRES OF LAND, more or less, in the County of Apache, State of Arizona; STATE OF ARIZONA, et al, and UNKNOWN OWNERS in "File for Section 2, T 19N, R 24E." Arizona State Land Department Archives, Phoenix, Arizona.

104. "Superintendent's Report for November 1962," December 13, 1962. PFNP Archives.

105. "Superintendent's Report for December 1962," January 11, 1963. PFNP Archives

106. See "Letter from W. W. McGrath, Director of Finance, Land Inventory Section to L. C. Duncan, Deputy Land Commissioner," September 21, 1970, in "File for Section 2, T 19N, R 24E." Arizona State Land Department Archives, Phoenix, Arizona. The receipt for the check is also in this file.

107. "Letter from Charles J. Smith, Superintendent, Petrified Forest National Monument to The Director of the National Park Service, July 2, 1934," in "File for Section 2, T 19N, R 24E." Arizona State Land Department Archives.

108. J. B. Jackson, "Other-Directed Houses," Landscape 6, no. 2 (Winter 1956–57): 29.

109. Rothman, Devil's Bargains, 40.

110. Ibid., 165.

111. The term "honky-tonk improvisations" is from Robert Venturi, Denise Scott Brown, and Steven Izenour in Learning from Las Vegas, rev. ed. (Cambridge, Mass.: MIT Press, 1977), 52.

ANNMARIE ADAMS

Sex and the Single Building

The Weston Havens House, 1941–2001

This study explores an iconic twentieth-century house, the Weston Havens house, (Figure 1) in Berkeley, California, designed by architect Harwell Hamilton Harris between 1939 and 1941. It was inspired by personal circumstances. After occupying his beloved "Sky House" for sixty years, philanthropist Weston Havens donated the famous house to the University of California in 2001.[1] As part of my planned sabbatical in Berkeley in 2007–2008, I was offered a chance to live in the Havens house. But when university representatives learned that I would be coming with a husband and two children, the offer was recanted: "The house won't work for a family," they said. Curious to know how an icon of postwar domestic architecture could not accommodate my family—which, I usually assume, is the conventional family size and organization meant to inhabit such houses—my interest was piqued. Why was this impossible? Could such a house exist? How queer.

What is queer space? Where does queer theory intersect architecture? Emerging in the early 1990s as both a challenge to and a subfield of gender and gay and lesbian studies, queer theory encompasses "whatever is at odds with the normal, the legitimate, the dominant. There is nothing in particular to which it necessarily refers. It is an identity without an essence."[2] While queer theory is most closely associated with literary criticism, relatively few scholars in architecture have explored queerness. Those who have studied queerness have mostly engaged a traditional definition of queer space, focusing on architecture that is occupied or created by gay or lesbian people.[3] A broader definition of queer space, drawing

on queer theory, would suggest that architecture that is itself odd or different might also qualify as queer space.

Still, architecture holds great potential in the explication of queerness because it is part of the constellation of forces that shape gender performance. As gender theorist Judith Butler explains, "there is no gender identity behind the expressions of gender; that identity is performatively constituted by the very 'expressions' that are said to be its results." Crucially, it is not space in general but spaces in particular that allow for and insist on different gendered possibilities.[4] The exploration of a "single building" then, such as the Weston Havens house, offers a particular example of queer space that allows us to rethink previous studies of queer architecture. It is also my contention that its pedigree as a work by Harris allowed for a kind of consensus of appreciation regarding the house that made it a significant architectural destination.

One of the challenges in this study is to mobilize the material evidence of photographs, architectural plans, drawings, the actual built structure, and written accounts, while never losing sight of the broader theoretical questions this remarkable building poses. In terms of methodologies, Bernard Herman's concept of "embedded landscapes," combining Ian Hodder's contextual archaeology and Dell Upton's experiential analysis, informs this reading of the house.[5] The premise is that like Herman's study of a typology (the Charleston single house), a concentrated focus on the plan can highlight a home's role in shaping the lived spatial experiences of actual people as they live out social roles through performances of gender. As material evidence of lived experience, the house and its contents reveal spatial relationships that encouraged certain social interactions, as well as particular socially constructed performances of the self, while making others spatially (and thus bodily) impossible. In this way, Butler's work helps us to think through and bring into representation these performances that might otherwise seem impossible within the architecture of normativity: the single-family home. Butler's theory thus serves to "queer" the methods we often engage for material culture studies.

Examining the building beyond Weston Havens's life span marks one of the project's contributions to vernacular architecture studies. As Upton's work reiterates, "the history of architecture should account for the *entire* life of a structure from its initial planning to its destruction and even its afterlife in history and myth."[6] Vernacularists have argued that the users and observers of architecture deserve attention in architectural history, alongside architects and builders. With this in mind, the eventual fate of the house as property of the University of California is an important part of its story. Weston Havens believed his house held important lessons for future architects. His private haven is now "public" property. This apparent contradiction casts new meaning on the house, perhaps linking it to Beatriz Colomina's compelling argument that modernity "coincides with the publicity of the private."[7]

More broadly speaking, this study brings sexuality to the attention of vernacularists. While the focus of the field has moved from a relatively exclusive focus on "common" buildings to a whole range of spaces, studies of sexuality and space are still notably absent in the literature from vernacular architecture studies. In Angel Kwolek-Folland's useful literature review of gender as an analytical category in vernacular architecture studies in 1995, she argues that gender studies could revolutionize the field, noting its negligible impact: "What is needed is the sense that gender *matters,* that it acts in powerful and compelling ways, that it can reveal important aspects of the history of the built environment

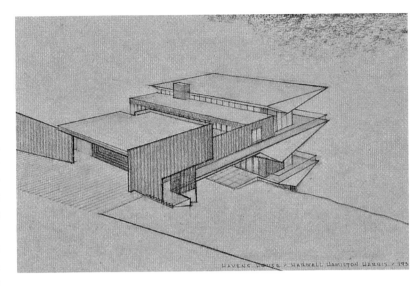

Figure 1. Axonometric drawing of the Weston Havens house by architect Harwell Hamilton Harris. Courtesy of Alexander Architectural Archive, the University of Texas at Austin.

that otherwise would go unexplored."[8] Nearly fifteen years later, with a burgeoning literature on gender and vernacular architecture as a foundation, we need to acknowledge that sexuality also matters.[9] We need to encourage students to think about the ways in which buildings reinforce heterosexuality as a social and cultural norm, and get them to think about the ways that scholarly discourse has often supported that cultural project by assuming that sexuality is not an issue.[10]

House Description

The Havens house is odd and different in many ways, including its siting. It is a two-story, flat-roofed, wooden house, comprised of two sections separated by a twenty-one-foot-long bridge. Unlike many other houses in the Berkeley hills, the house is fully detached from its steep site.[11] Whereas most houses set in the city's steep slopes facing San Francisco and its bay are dug into the ground, the main section of the Havens house steps out away from its steep site and toward the view.

The structure of the six-thousand-square-foot, redwood-clad house combines ubiquitous Californian balloon framing topped by unusual inverted wood trusses. Architectural historian John Loomis has noted that like buildings designed by Frank Lloyd Wright, Richard Neutra, and Rudolph Schindler, it follows a three-foot grid.[12] What are particularly striking about the

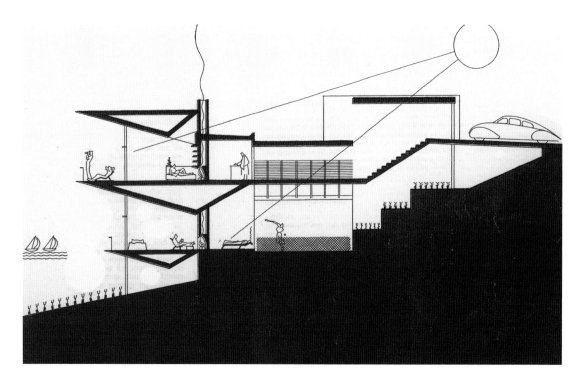

structure of the house are the inverted gables, "almost as if a series of gables had been turned upside down," which also define the sloping ceilings inside, further projecting the occupant's view toward the sky and bay.[13] These unusual trusses not only support the loads of the building itself but also its innovative heating system. Each inverted gable serves as a "plenum chamber," radiating heat downward onto the inhabitants.[14]

From the street, the three-bedroom house unfolds in a series of carefully choreographed steps toward San Francisco Bay, building tension followed by sudden release. A discreet opening in a seven-foot wall at 255 Panoramic Way leads to a stairway and the long, covered bridge that runs below street level; the real entrance to the house then gives onto a two-story block distinguished by this structure of inverted gables that directs the views to San Francisco Bay and also to the glorious California sky (Figure 2). Entry to the house per se is almost startling, with a spectacularly open, combined living and dining room. This generous and brightly lit room is approximately 15 x 15 feet. Ten-foot-high, floor-to-ceiling glass fenestration gives onto a continuous, sixty-five-foot-wide deck with chain-link fence, facing the bay. While approximately two-thirds of the

room is intended as the living room, with a brick fireplace, built-in seating, stereo equipment, and grand piano, the remaining space is for dining. A strategically placed five-foot-wide wooden closet, marking the axial entrance from the bridge, subtly divides the grand space. Among Harris's papers at the University of Texas at Austin is an elongated perspective of this unique room (Figure 3) in which the architect omitted the glass between the interior and exterior terrace, shown only near the roof. The folding partition in the dining room behind the table is a pass-through to the kitchen. In Harris's perspective it is shown with a cloud pattern, but in the actual house this partition is decorated with a map of the world without national boundaries, painted by Patricia Fudger.

In terms of its plan, the main floor (at the level of the entry bridge) contains a housekeeper's room and laundry room in the section nearest the street. The main block of the house is the kitchen, dining/living room, and a bedroom and bathroom accessible from a curved hallway separated from the entry sequence by a door. A dramatic spiral stairway, adjacent to the entry, leads downstairs to two bedrooms with en suite bathrooms facing private terraces (separated by

Figure 3. Harris's perspective of living and dining room omitted the glass between the interior and exterior terrace. Courtesy of Alexander Architectural Archive, the University of Texas at Austin.

the stairway) that look onto a large courtyard and terraced garden.

The Protagonists

Havens was the last in the line of one of Berkeley's founders, Francis Kittredge Shattuck, and he spent his life as a quiet patron of the arts, managing his family's assets. He graduated in 1923 from the University of California at Berkeley with a degree in economics and then spent a year studying English literature as a graduate student. Havens traveled extensively and indulged his deep interests in the visual arts. According to Loomis, on a trip to Europe in 1938 he met Le Corbusier and was particularly inspired by the work of Alvar Aalto. On his return to Berkeley, he purchased the property at 255 Panoramic Way and hired Los Angeles-based architect Harwell Hamilton Harris to design him a house.[15] He was never married and never discussed his sexual orientation (purportedly gay). His fortune is now the Weston Havens Foundation, which mostly funds medical research. His personal library, still in the house today, includes many architectural books.

Harris was interested in architecture from an early age, both in practice and in academia. According to the architect's biographer Lisa Germany, this interest stemmed from his architect-father, Fred Harris.[16] Harwell was largely self-taught and worked as an apprentice for Richard Neutra (1929–1931) and Rudolph Schindler (1931–1932).[17] Harris's career took a sudden turn in 1951, when he became the dean at the University of Texas. For the next four years he presided over a group of innovative young educators, known as the "Texas Rangers," who revolutionized early design education. Nevertheless, these years were marked by frustration and regret, and he resigned in 1955.[18]

Nonhierarchical Space

If we turn attention from the biographical/social to the architectural evidence of the Havens house, three themes contribute to a nascent understanding of queer architecture. The first two come directly from the house plan: (1) the arrangement of bedrooms in the Havens house is nonhierarchical; (2) the house is about secrecy and invisibility; (3) at the same time, the house is a public spectacle.

I speculate that the existence of nonhierarchical bedrooms in the Havens house is why university officials believed we couldn't live there. While most postwar, upper middle-class, suburban

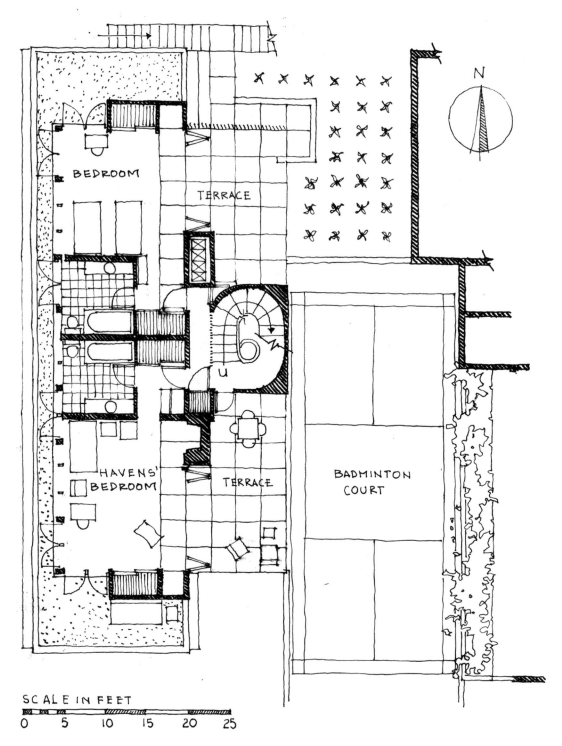

Figure 4. Lower level plan of the Weston Havens house, Berkeley, California, published in *Architectural Forum* in September 1943. Redrawn by Carlos Rueda.

BEDROOM

TERRACE

HAVENS' BEDROOM

TERRACE

BADMINTON COURT

N

SCALE IN FEET

0   5   10   15   20   25

architect–designed houses would echo the power and age hierarchy of parents and children—the so-called master bedroom almost always larger than the others and often with its own bathroom—the Havens house has three large, nearly equal, and secluded bedrooms, in addition to a smaller bedroom for a housekeeper, located near the entry. That is, it has three so-called master bedrooms. As the plans illustrate (Figures 4 and 5), the circulation of the house is such that each bedroom is entirely separated from the others, and the cluster of baths and closets between the two bedrooms on the lower level functions as a sound barrier. These closets thus served as significant spaces in the house, not only as storage space but also with a sociological and technological function, to separate people and muffle sounds. Havens occupied the south bedroom on the lower level, subtly differentiated from the others by its slightly larger size and the inclusion of the fireplace.[19]

Other houses designed by Harris for unmarried clients, another form of the "single building," do not show this same equality in the design of the bedrooms nor the urge to isolate bedrooms. Clearly, the unusual bedroom arrangement wasn't about living alone. The Helene Kershner house Harris designed in Los Angeles in 1935, for example, had two very different bedrooms on the upper floor (i.e., one had a dressing room and en suite bath). The weekend house for Marion Clark at Carmel-by-the-Sea in 1937 also had two distinctly unequal bedrooms. One faces the street while the other one is larger, includes a private bathroom with a tub, and has a spectacular view of the Pacific Ocean.[20]

The three main bedrooms at the Havens house face onto what Max Jacobson, Murray Silverstein, and Barbara Winslow call "the secret heart of the house," a 945-square-foot courtyard that was apparently intended for badminton.[21] According to the extant correspondence between the architect and his client, Havens demanded the badminton court from the very beginning of the project: "As you remember, there were two basic requirements when the plan began. First, the house must be high enough to look over the adjoining house. Second, there must be a badminton court on the east," writes Jean Murray Bangs, the wife of Harwell Harris, in June 1940.[22] Although other homes of the interwar era that served this social class often included recreational or gymlike spaces, a badminton court is atypical. Was Havens a badminton player or an observer? Why not a secret swimming pool? Because the three bedrooms are the only interior spaces that look over the court, this shared view unites them in purpose and underlines their nonhierarchical character.

Cave for Moles

The Havens house offers several metaphors to describe queer space. Harris called the house "A

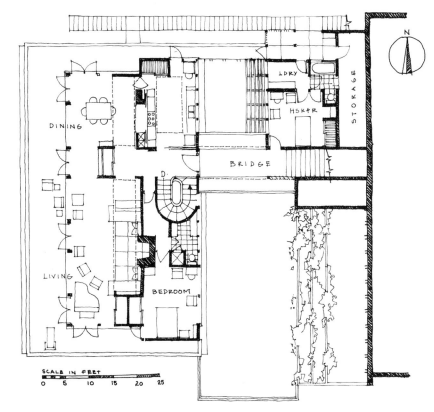

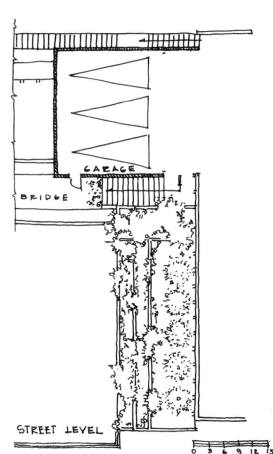

Figure 5. Upper level plan and street level plan of the Weston Havens house, Berkeley, California, published by *Architectural Forum* in September 1943. Redrawn by Carlos Rueda.

Figure 6. Harris described the Havens house as "a cave . . . for moles." He published a photograph of this room in *Harwell Hamilton Harris: A Collection of His Writings and Buildings* in 1965. Photograph by Annmarie Adams.

cave . . . for moles" in a caption showing a photograph (Figure 6) of the living room published in 1965, comparing the structure to the solitary, nearly invisible burrows where moles live.[23] The popular metaphor of the closet to stand for hidden homosexuality, then, is augmented here by the image of the mole in the cave. If the closet is a mere fragment of a house to which the queer figure retreats, the cave is rather the actual home of the mole in which a much grander and yet more secret life is lived. If the closet implies repression, the mole's cave suggests a certain comfort in isolation.

While the Havens house is located wholly above grade, it is a secret architecture with few traces to betray its internal organization from the street. Note that this goes against two typical modernist ideas: the blurring of inside and out and the legibility of the building's organization from the exterior.[24] Indeed, the sequence in which the house unfolds is all about discreet obstacles.[25] From Panoramic Way the view of the house is blocked by the unadorned wall, giving little sense of the sunken badminton court just

behind it; on entering the nearly invisible gate, the house blocks the view of the bay; along the covered bridge, the view down into the badminton court is partially blocked by angled louvers and deep shelves for plants. The climax is in the living room, where the Golden Gate Bridge is seen in perfect elevation.

Many other authors who have explored queer space have noted the importance of secrecy, especially through the idea of the closet. Aaron Betsky, in his 1997 book *Queer Space,* says the three main elements of queer space are the closet, the mirror, and the orgasm. Betsky's closet is a dark, musty, disorderly place, offering its user the "building blocks for the person you become in the real world. It is also a place where you return to your body."[26] Perhaps following Eve Sedgewick's much-cited *Epistemology of the Closet* (1990), most secondary literature in architecture dealing with queer space either focuses on the metaphor of the closet as disguise or as a metaphor of homosexual oppression: "The closet is the defining structure for gay oppression in this century."[27]

Both Betsky and Henry Urbach, author of an influential article on the metaphor of the closet, note the nearly equal importance of display or mirrors to places they consider queer. Other sensorial experiences, such as sound, temperature, humidity, and smell, rarely enter the equation. The Havens house marks an addition to thinking about queer space because it forces reflection on senses beyond vision—especially touch, whose receptors are located all over the body.[28] The innovative heating system is one way in which the Havens house forces reflection on touch.

This is one advantage of the "embedded landscapes" approach. Upton has noted the importance of our embodied experience of all buildings and cities—what he refers to as the entire built environment or cultural landscape. "It is experiential," he explains, "because metaphors and analogies acquire their force through our corporeal participation in our surroundings."[29] The Havens house heating system is a good example of such corporeal participation. A double page (Figure 7) of *Architectural Forum* from 1943 reveals its integral design, whereby warm air is transported by pipes into the triangular, hollow ceiling sections.[30] The heat is then radiated down onto the inhabitants, just like real sunshine, and high temperatures are intended to be offset by cooling bay breezes that enter through the ever-open expanses of glass that wrap the house. It is an extremely luxurious system, designed for a specific body effect: a constant cycle of warmed skin cooled by fresh air. Thus the heating system created an artificial environment mimicking the effects of sunlight that would allow the mole, Havens, to remain comfortable in his cave.

Can we imagine the badminton court as a space akin to Urbach's ante-closet, the space in front of the closet? As Urbach explains:

The ante-closet has a curious status in architectural drawings, conventionally rendered as a kind of graphic interruption. The notation for "door swing" is an arc that traces the passage of the unhinged edge from open to shut. Whether drawn as a light solid line or a series of dashed segments, this arc does not indicate, as other lines do, "cut" material. Instead, it records the possibility of architectural

movement, of changing spatial relations. At once conventional and incredibly bizarre, a moment of graphic folding, the notation for "door swing" registers the making and unmaking of architectural space.[31]

As a highly unusual space without a clear domestic function, the badminton court was a space of ambiguity and/or multiplicity, a site of escape from normativity.[32] Indeed, Havens's badminton court is like Urbach's ante-closet, the intimate space before the storage space sometimes used for primping and self-admiration: "a space that emerges, both within and against social relations, to constitute a space of self-representation at once connected to and free from social norms."[33]

Were the cavelike bedrooms for guests? It is here that Alice Friedman's insightful comparison of the Farnsworth house and the Johnson house in terms of gender, sexuality, and privacy helps us to understand the Havens house. In chapter 4 of *Women and the Making of the Modern House*, entitled "People Who Live in Glass Houses,"

Figure 7. This detailed cross section shows the integral heating and ventilation system of the Weston Havens house. It was published in *Architectural Forum* in September 1943. Redrawn by Carlos Rueda.

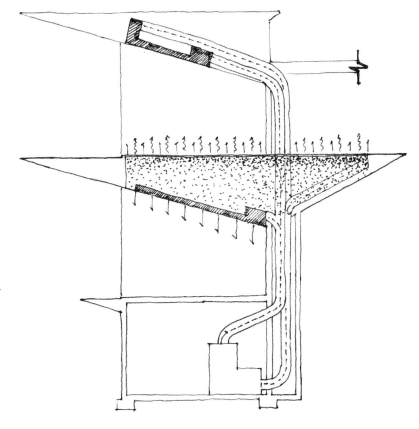

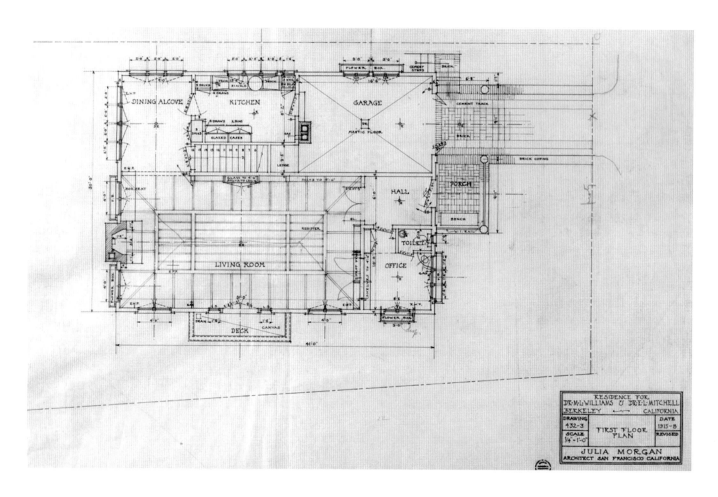

Figure 8. Architect
Julia Morgan located
physicians Clara Williams
and Elsie Mitchell's
medical office at the
entrance to their shared
residence at the front
door, foreshadowing
how gay homes would
be described nearly a
century later. Courtesy of
Environmental Design
Archives, University of
California, Berkeley.

Friedman compares single woman doctor Edith Farnsworth's disappointment with her Plano, Illinois, glass house to gay New York architect Philip Johnson's pleasure in his glass house in New Canaan, Connecticut. Friedman describes a rich underground culture developed by gay and lesbian Americans in an attempt to "appear normal," focusing on camp culture as a strategy for Johnson in particular.[34] Like the Havens house, the Johnson house relied on a series of architectural devices that screened, distorted, and denied visual access to the house. Friedman also elucidates what she calls "the double-sided nature of domestic life" for gay men.[35] She contrasts the theatrical transparency of the glass house with the opacity of the nearby guest house: "a windowless bunker, a defensible space of intimacy as well as a closet containing the unseen apparel of a gay man's life," recalling Betsky's closet/mirror and Urbach's insistence on simultaneous concealment and disclosure.[36] Friedman's unforgettable interpretation of the Farnsworth

house also helps us to understand the Havens house by pointing out the mid-century American public's general discomfort with unmarried people. Mies apparently included a guest bathroom in the Farnsworth house, for example, in order to keep visitors from "seeing Edith's nightgown on the back of the bathroom door."[37] Like Farnsworth's "homeliness" and/or her age and physical appearance, constantly noted by historians, a glimpse of her nightgown would have pointed to her solitary lifestyle.[38]

Purpose-built, queer, domestic architecture, designed by famous architects and with this same double-sidedness, can be found in Berkeley two generations before the Havens house or the Johnson house. An example is the 1915 house designed by Julia Morgan for physicians Clara Williams and Elsie Mitchell (Figure 8). The bedrooms are all on the lower level, and at the heart of the house is a magnificent living room. Doctors Williams and Mitchell shared a medical office, located immediately inside the front door, disguising their domestic partnership in the same way Urbach has noted that the homes of gay couples today are often purposefully camouflaged by professional partnerships in architectural and lifestyle publications. "Since the couples are also business associates" says Urbach, "the articles can and, without exception do avoid the words lover, domestic partner, companion and boy/girlfriend."[39] Despite a completely different historical context, this Morgan house plan shows that same idea by putting the medical office up front and disguising the stair down to the bedrooms, which logically would have been placed at the front door. The Havens house, with its three nearly identical bedrooms, presents a similarly ambiguous situation, though admittedly without the camouflaging effect of a second inhabitant.

Urbach also notes in the same article the tendency for gay and lesbian couples' houses to present an array of bedrooms without any particular clues as to who sleeps where: "Gay couples . . . always have multiple bedrooms that seem to belong to no one in particular. The history, nature and texture of a gay relationship is consistently overlooked and ignored. As a result, the design of gay homes cannot be depicted as an expression of personality and lifestyle. Decor becomes, instead, a metonym for undisclosed lives."[40] The three bedrooms in the Havens house are nearly equal in size, view, and washroom facilities; all three, interestingly enough, face the so-called badminton court. Urbach's insight about ambiguous bedroom assignments thus resonates with both the themes of the nonhierarchical bedrooms and their secret disposition. The adult-only bedrooms in the Havens house, looking onto a shared, ambivalent, discreet space (the badminton court) functions in direct opposition to the plans of most postwar, middle-class houses, where the parents' and children's rooms occupy a separate, "nighttime" zone and often look onto distinct areas of a yard or lawn, visible from the neighbors' houses and/or sometimes the street.

House for Eagles

At the same time that the sleeping spaces inside the Havens house were opaque and controlled, it was also a carefully choreographed public spectacle on the exterior. Clearly the Havens house displays the same double-sidedness as Friedman notes in Johnson's simultaneously transparent and opaque houses. In the same publication where Harris called the Havens house a cave for moles, he described the building as "a sky house . . . for eagles."[41] Always more interested in the formal relationships than theoretical ones, Harris may have been referring to the way the inverted gables of the house made it appear to be poised in flight, propelling visitors skyward like an eagle. In another situation Harris said the house "does not frame the view, it projects the beholder into it," reiterating this metaphor of propulsion.[42] The building poised in flight is certainly the theme of Man Ray's famous photograph of the Weston Havens house, taken in 1941 (Figure 9).

The eagle's perch that contributes to an understanding of the house as queer space, however, is the visibility of the building in publications. The Havens house was published even before it was finished.[43] A section of the house graced the cover of *California Arts and Architecture* in March 1940 (see Figure 2). This highly stylized drawing shows a single male figure in seven different poses: preparing food, reading beside the fireplace, reclining on the deck, and photographing the view; downstairs, the same man reads in a bedroom, sun bathes on the private terrace, and plays a vigorous game of tennis, rather than badminton. A model of the house was exhibited at the New York Architectural League during the same month, and a photograph of the model appeared in *Architectural Record* in April. Bangs was particularly keen on documenting the construction process of the house, too. She wrote in an undated letter to Havens:

> Since your house is to be "one of the really important modern houses in America," I quote Mr. Edward Kaufman Jr., we ought to have a record of its construction [. . .] A slow motion camera is planted on the job and runs continuously during the most important parts of the construction like the framing. Then when the film is run off the house is built before your eyes. Wouldn't that be fun? Think of it showing at the Museum of Modern Art?[44]

Bangs also showed the drawings of the house to visitors to the architectural office: "By the way, Noyes of the Museum of Modern Art and young Kaufman of Pittsburgh (Wright's Falling Water house) were in yesterday and admired the plans of your house."[45]

Perhaps due to this advance publicity, the house quickly became a tourist attraction. It was featured in a now-lost 16mm documentary film commissioned by Havens and made by Erven Jourdan (music by Manuel Compinsky; Harris provided animation drawings). It was featured in *Life* magazine (1949)[46] and appeared on a list of fourteen significant buildings in America since 1907, nominated by *Architectural Record* (1957).[47] Eventually the house was donated to a public university.[48] Now visiting architecture professors stay in it for a night or a semester, almost like a hotel, and a generation of architecture students are taken to the house on field trips. That Weston Havens wanted his ultraprivate sanctuary—his

mole cave, to use Harris's term—to become well known, well viewed, and public property is surprising and at first glance seems contradictory to the architect's multiple and sophisticated attempts to make the house appear and feel "secret."

I contend, then, that purpose-built, mid-century queer space hovers somewhere between a space that is invisible, almost fortified, certainly unspoken, and one that's virtually transparent, a household world. The publication of the Havens house photographs, such as those taken by Man Ray and others published in *House Beautiful* in 1944, led to its remarkable popularity as a tourist attraction.[49] Such publicity in the popular press blurred conventional definitions of manhood by associating the iconic house with its client, emphasizing his role as a decorator and arranger of domestic space—roles associated with women.[50] Havens's deep interest in the decorative arts is evident in his frequent letters to and from

Figure 9. Man Ray's famous photograph of the Weston Havens house emphasized the metaphor of flight. Copyright Man Ray Trust / SODRAC, 2009.

Bangs.[51] Reminiscent of the casual and abbreviated tones we use for email and texting today, Mr. Havens and Mrs. Harris refer to each other by pet names, and their correspondence constitutes a lively sometimes cynical but certainly humorous two-way conversation. "Panoramic job still moving with usual inefficiency . . . hardware situation in complete mess countless problems lying dormant awaiting your arrival,"[52] telegrammed Havens to Bangs in mid-June 1941 regarding his twenty-four-thousand-dollar home.[53]

Besides their chummy relationship, what is very clear from the correspondence is the degree of responsibility Bangs took for design decisions, in addition to typing her husband's correspondence. The hundreds of letters in the Alexander Architectural Archive at the University of Texas at Austin show her involvement in every detail, but especially in placating the client.

Indeed, letters are crucial evidence of a deep connection between the house and an admiring public that passes over Havens's personal life. Without the personal testimony of Havens himself, among the most important sources for this paper is a handful of letters sent to Havens from a wide range of individuals who toured the house and then thanked their host for the opportunity. The letters, preserved today in the Environmental Design Archives at the University of California at Berkeley, reinforce this paradox of an extremely private life brilliantly concealed within the publicity for a very public house. Most letter writers did not even know Havens's name, but they knew his house. "I am terribly sorry for having had to address you in this impersonal way but, not knowing your name, it seemed like the only feasible way," confessed Professor Neil Levine of Harvard University in 1976.[54] A particularly revealing source among the extant letters is an exquisite drawing of the house on the envelope, as a clue to the delivery person (Figure 10). The letter writer knew Havens's name—it's a thank-you note and a rather gutsy critique of his color schemes—but not the street or the address.

Following most visits, grateful correspondents compared the house to other tourist attractions: "even Big Sur did not overshadow our visit with you," wrote Louise Andrews after seeing the house with her husband, Michael.[55] "I think I

Figure 10. This Seattle-based visitor to the Havens house included a drawing of the building instead of its address. Mary Bassetti to Weston Havens, February 7, 1947. Courtesy of Environmental Design Archives, University of California, Berkele

realize the bother you are put to so the thank you is doubly meant. It is very beautiful," wrote Dean William Wurster to Havens in 1950.[56] The architect himself wrote to his former client in 1989, using his code name for the skybound house, Havens Above: "Havens Above seems to attrack [sic] more visitors as the years to [sic] by. I hope they are not a nuisance," wrote an eighty-six-year-old Harwell Hamilton Harris from Raleigh, North Carolina.[57] Might these last two letters evince a post-Stonewall self-consciousness about Havens's private life? Can we imagine them as examples of people who, in 1986, could read the code of the mole that was unbreakable to all but the initiated in 1946? There is even a sense from the letters that the house stood in for Havens's personality: "Because we were so overwhelmed by your house, we didn't ask you much about yourself. I wish we had," confessed Frank Harmon in 1986.[58] The double-sidedness of the design was also noted by visitors. In 1986, John Dixon, who was a professor of religion and art at University of North Carolina, remarked in his thank-you letter to Havens, "I had no idea of . . . how private and intimate parts of the house could be in contrast to the majesty of the public spaces. It is a splendid example of living in the best of different worlds."[59]

Conclusion

To this day, the Weston Havens house is a public performance of Havens's private life, propelled by his efforts to publicize his house through film, print media, and architectural tourism. The three main bedrooms in the house are remarkably similar, with a notable resistance to the typical arrangement of one dominating the others, such as in a standard master bedroom arrangement. Secondly, every scale of the house functions as a discreet obstacle, reinforcing Havens's desire for an ultraprivate, cavelike realm. And thirdly, Havens publicized and maintained control of this secret, domestic world by welcoming visitors and journalists, by commissioning a film about the house, and finally by donating it to a state university.

Following Butler's theory of gender performativity, correspondence between Havens and Harris's wife, Jean Murray Bangs, letters to Havens from grateful visitors, and various magazine articles underline how the Weston Havens house occupied an overlapping space between queer space and dominant, normative space. The house managed to operate within a specific type of architectural visibility, even as it masked, screened, and protected the identity and activities of the inhabitants. This "passing" is what is so fascinating about the Weston Havens house. The architectural beauty of the house, as well as its pedigree as a work by Harris, allowed the anomalies of the house, its "queerness," to come out.

NOTES

Thanks to two anonymous readers, Elizabeth Byrne, Greig Crysler, Miranda Hambro, John Loomis, Waverly Lowell, Eliahu Perszyk, Carlos Rueda, Nancy Sparrow, and Abigail Van Slyck. I am particularly grateful to Cynthia Hammond, Silvia Spampinato, David Theodore, and Julia Tischer for their creative contributions to this paper. I also acknowledge the support of the Arcus Foundation and the students of ARCH 279X, Sex and the Single Building, at the University of California in spring 2008.

1. John A. Loomis, "UC Berkeley Gets Havens House," *Architecture* 92, no. 9 (September 2003): 21.

2. David Halperin, *Saint Foucault: Towards a Gay Hagiography* (New York: Oxford University Press, 1997), 63. Also cited in Nikki Sullivan, *A Critical Introduction to Queer Theory* (New York: New York University Press, 2003), 43.

3. Major publications on space and same-sex desire are Aaron Betsky, *Queer Space: Architecture and Same-sex Desire* (New York: William Morrow, 1997); Henry Urbach, "Closets, Clothes, DisClosure," *Assemblage* 30 (Aug. 1996): 62–73; Katarina Bonnevier, "A Queer Analysis of Eileen Gray's E. 1027," in *Negotiating Domesticity: Spatial Productions of Gender in Modern Architecture,* ed. Hilde Heynen and Gulsum Baydar, 162–80 (London: Routledge, 2005); Alice T. Friedman, "People Who Live in Glass Houses: Edith Farnsworth, Ludwig Mies van der Rohe, and Philip Johnson," in *Women and the Making of the Modern House* (New Haven, Conn.: Yale University Press, 2007), 126–59; and George Wagner, "The Lair of the Bachelor" in *Architecture and Feminism,* ed. Debra Coleman et al., 183–220 (New York: Princeton Architectural Press, 1996).

4. Judith Butler, *Gender Trouble: Feminism and the Subversion of Identity* (New York: Routledge, 1999), 33. Two scholars who discuss Butler's performativity in regard to architecture are Hilda Heynan, "Modernity and Domesticity: Tensions and Contradictions," in *Negotiating Domesticity: Spatial Productions of Gender in Modern Architecture,* ed. Hilde Heynen and Gulsum Baydar, 1–29 (London: Routledge, 2005); and Katarina Bonnevier, *Behind Straight Curtains: Towards a Queer Feminist Theory of Architecture* (Stockholm: Axl Books, 2007).

5. Bernard L. Herman, "The Embedded Landscapes of the Charleston Single House, 1780–1820," *Exploring Everyday Landscapes: Perspectives in Vernacular Architecture 7,* ed. Annmarie Adams and Sally McMurry, 41–57 (Knoxville: University of Tennessee Press, 1997); Dell Upton, "White and Black Landscapes in Eighteenth-Century Virginia," *Places* 2, no. 2 (1984): 59–72; Dell Upton, *Holy Things and Profane: Anglican Parish Churches in Colonial Virginia* (New York: Architectural History Foundation, 1986), 205–19; Ian Hodder, *Reading the Past: Current Approaches to Interpretation in Archaeology* (Cambridge: Cambridge University Press, 1986), 118–46.

6. Dell Upton, *Architecture of the United States* (Oxford: Oxford University Press, 1998), 12.

7. Beatriz Colomina, *Privacy and Publicity: Modern Architecture as Mass Media* (Cambridge, Mass.: MIT Press, 1994), 9.

8. Angel Kwolek-Folland, "Gender as a Category of Analysis in Vernacular Architecture Studies," *Gender, Class, and Shelter: Perspectives in Vernacular Architecture V*, ed. Elizabeth Collins Cromley and Carter L. Hudgins (Knoxville: University of Tennessee Press, 1995), 8.

9. Studies of ordinary places that oppress women include Marion Roberts, *Living in a Man-Made World: Gender Assumptions in Modern Housing Design* (London: Routledge, 1991); Daphne Spain, *Gendered Spaces* (Chapel Hill: University of North Carolina Press, 1992); Leslie Kanes Weisman, *Discrimination by Design: A Feminist Critique of the Man-Made Environment* (Urbana: University of Illinois Press, 1992). On how architecture shapes gender roles, see Annmarie Adams, *Architecture in the Family Way: Doctors, Women, and Housing, 1870–1900* (Montreal: McGill-Queen's University Press, 1996); Annmarie Adams, "The Eichler Home: Intention and Experience in Postwar Suburbia," *Gender, Class, and Shelter: Perspectives in Vernacular Architecture V*, ed. Elizabeth Collins Cromley and Carter L. Hudgins, 164–78 (Knoxville: University of Tennessee Press, 1995); Dolores Hayden, *The Grand Domestic Revolution: A History of Feminist Designs in American Homes, Neighborhoods, and Cities* (Cambridge, Mass.: MIT Press, 1981); Gwendolyn Wright, *Moralism and the Model Home: Domestic Architecture and Cultural Conflict in Chicago, 1873–1913* (Chicago: University of Chicago Press, 1980).

10. I am grateful to Abigail Van Slyck for this insight, especially for pointing out how scholarly discourse supports patriarchy by assuming that gender is not an issue in building design. Personal correspondence, January 9, 2008.

11. The only real visual connection of the house to the slope is its retaining wall and planter boxes. See *Architectural Forum* 9 (September 1943): 80.

12. Germany claims that Harris discovered the benefits of the three-foot grid with the Lowe house. See Lisa Germany, *Harwell Hamilton Harris* (Berkeley and Los Angeles: University of California Press, 2000), 45. Also see John A. Loomis, "House on the Hill," *San Francisco Chronicle*, July 17, 2004, sec. F-1.

13. *The Studio* 128, no. 616 (July 1944): 101.

14. Germany, *Harwell Hamilton Harris*, 86.

15. Biographical information comes from John Loomis's unpublished book on the house, "HAVENS—HOUSE—HARRIS: The Weston Havens House by Harwell Hamilton Harris," 9–10.

16. Germany, *Harwell Hamilton Harris*, 1–13.

17. Loomis, "HAVENS—HOUSE—HARRIS," 11–12.

18. John A. Loomis, "Power Rangers," *Design Book Review* 40 (Fall 1999): 62–69. He characterizes Harris's changed reputation, following his move to academia, using the French term *le second couteau*, the second knife (roughly equivalent to second fiddle or second string in English). From 1962 until the time of his death in 1990, claims Loomis, "Harris had little of the drive that had marked his youth."

19. On the detailed plans of the Havens house published by *House Beautiful* in 1944, the southern room on the lower level is labelled "Owner's Room." See "How to Judge Modern," *House Beautiful* (August 1944): 52.

20. Harris may also have designed houses for other unmarried men. These houses are cited as examples because their single clients were easy to identify in Lisa Germany's list of clients' names.

21. Max Jacobson et al., *The Good House: Contrast as a Design Tool* (Newtown, Conn.: Taunton Press, 1990), 100.

22. Personal correspondence from Jean Murray Bangs to Weston Havens, June 3, 1940. Alexander Architectural Archive, the University of Texas at Austin (Box 27, Folder 8).

23. Harwell Hamilton Harris, *Harwell Hamilton Harris: A Collection of His Writings and Buildings* (Raleigh: Student Publication of the School of Design, University of North Carolina, 1965), 48–49.

24. Beatriz Colomina points out that Adolf Loos's houses offered a convoluted distinction between exterior and interior, as the spaces encourage users to face the space they have just transgressed, and furniture is placed to force users' views inwards. See Colomina, *Privacy and Publicity*, 233–81.

25. Two queer readings of Eileen Gray's E. 1027 house engage this same approach. Jasmine Rault's doctoral dissertation shows how Gray resisted certain modernist norms and strategically deployed barriers and obstacles to visual dominance within the living space. See Jasmine Rault, "Eileen Gray: New Angles on Gender and Sexuality," (PhD diss., McGill University, 2006) and Bonnevier in *Negotiating Domesticity*, 162–80.

26. Betsky, *Queer Space: Architecture and Same-Sex Desire*, 17.

27. Eve Kosofsky Sedgwick, *Epistemology of the Closet* (Berkeley and Los Angeles: University of California Press, 1990), 71.

28. Diana Fuss makes a powerful case for the inclusion of sensorial experiences in architectural analyses, in *The Sense of an Interior: Four Writers and the Rooms That Shaped Them* (New York: Routledge, 2004).

29. Dell Upton, *Another City: Urban Life and Urban Spaces in the New American Republic* (New Haven, Conn.: Yale University Press, 2008), 12.

30. "Hillside House for Weston Havens," *Architectural Forum* 9 (September 1943): 86–87.

31. Urbach, "Closets, Clothes, DisClosure," 72.

32. I am grateful to Cynthia Hammond for this idea. She is using it in a forthcoming paper to look at spaces of ambiguity in terms of dissatisfaction with modernism, based on the presentation "'I Weep for Women': The *Home '53* Design Competition," Canadian Women Artists History Initiative Inaugural Conference, Concordia University, Montreal, October 4, 2008.

33. Urbach, "Closets, Clothes, DisClosure," 70.

34. Friedman, *Women and the Making of the Modern House*, 153.

35. Ibid., 152.

36. Ibid., 153.

37. Ibid., 143.

38. Franz Schulze, for example, describes Mies's client as a woman "whose formidable intellect compensated, but never enough, for a tall ungainly physical presence." See Franz Schulze, *The Farnsworth House* (Chicago: Lohan Associates, 1997), 12.

39. Henry Urbach, "Peeking at Gay Interiors," *Design Book Review* 25 (1992): 39.

40. Urbach, "Peeking at Gay Interiors," 38.

41. Harris, *Harwell Hamilton Harris*, 46.

42. *Architectural Forum* 9, 78.

43. According to the "Chronological Record of Principle Transactions," the drawings and specifications of the Havens house were issued for bidding on April 29, 1940.

44. Personal correspondence from Jean Murray Bangs to Weston Havens (n.d.). Alexander Architectural Archive, the University of Texas at Austin (Box 27, Folder 8).

45. Personal correspondence from Jean Murray Bangs to Weston Havens, July 10, 1940. Alexander Architectural Archive, the University of Texas at Austin (Box 27, Folder 8).

46. "San Francisco Houses," *Life* (September 5, 1949): 44–63.

47. "One Hundred Years of Significant Building," *Architectural Record* 121 (February 1957), 199–206.

48. Loomis, "UC Berkeley Gets Havens House," 21.

49. "How to Judge Modern," *House Beautiful*, 49–57, 70–71.

50. See Judy Attfield and Pat Kirkham, ed., *A View from the Interior: Women and Design* (London: Women's Press, 1989).

51. As Peter McNeil points out, it was not unusual for men to have an interest in flowers, decorative arts, and entertaining in the interwar period. Peter McNeil, "Crafting Queer Spaces: Privacy and Posturing," paper presented at the conference Queer Spaces: Centres and Peripheries, University of Technology Sydney, February 20–21, 2007, http://www.dab.uts.edu.au/conferences/queer_space/proceedings/cities_mcneil.pdf (accessed January 6, 2010).

52. Telegram from Weston Havens to Jean Murray Bangs, June 12, 1941. Alexander Architectural Archive, the University of Texas at Austin (Box 27, Folder 8).

53. According to the "Statement of Account and Certificate of Payment" issued on December 29, 1941, the original contract sum for the construction of the house was $24,790.00 and was increased to $30,659.86 on August 27, 1941. Certificate No. 7, December 29, 1941. Alexander Architectural Archive, the University of Texas at Austin (Box 27, Folder 6).

54. Personal correspondence from Professor Neil Levine to Weston Havens, July 6, 1976. Environmental Design Archives, University of California, Berkeley.

55. Personal correspondence from Louise Andrews to Weston Havens, August 6 (no year). Environmental Design Archives, University of California, Berkeley.

56. Personal correspondence from William W. Wurster to Weston Havens, August 14, 1950. Environmental Design Archives, University of California, Berkeley.

57. Personal correspondence from Harwell H. Harris to Weston Havens, April 25, 1989. Environmental Design Archives, University of California, Berkeley.

58. Personal correspondence from Frank Harmon to Weston Havens, November 3, 1986. Environmental

Design Archives, University of California, Berkeley.

59. Personal correspondence from John W. Dixon Jr. to Weston Havens, January 24, 1986. Environmental Design Archives, University of California, Berkeley.

Book Reviews

Anna Vemer Andrzejewski
Building Power: Architecture and Surveillance in Victorian America

Knoxville: University of Tennessee Press, 2008.
272 pages. 77 illustrations.
ISBN 1-57233-631-5, $39.00 HB

Review by Elaine Jackson-Retondo

More than three decades after the English translation of Michel Foucault's *Surveiller et Punir; Naissance de la Prison* was published in the United States *(Discipline and Punish: The Birth of the Prison)*, the nature of power and the discourse and the role of discipline and surveillance in modern society posited by Foucault continue to frame scholarly discussion and debate in a range of fields. Anna Vemer Andrzejewski's *Building Power* is one of the latest works in the field of architectural history to engage Foucault's study. Andrzejewski offers a breadth of particularity to the scholarly study of surveillance and discourse.

Andrzejewski steps outside the realm of penal institutions to examine how and to what degree surveillance and discourse inform the design and use of space in different building types from the mid-nineteenth through the early twentieth centuries in the United States. While Andrzejewski uses building types to ground her study in specific spaces in the Victorian United States, the crux of her analysis rests on types, or what Andrzejewski terms the "dominant intent" of surveillance. She argues that the dominant intent of surveillance and discourse determines the role surveillance plays in the design and use of space, as well as how surveillance is physically incor-

porated into a particular building or space, resulting in multifarious manifestations of surveillance. In other words, the dominant intent and discourse, not the building type, are the primary factors that inform specific surveillance techniques.

Andrzejewski selects four dominant intents to organize the main chapters of her book—discipline, efficiency, hierarchy, and fellowship. The framework further emphasizes that the primary subject of her study is the varied use and forms of surveillance rather than specific building types in which they were implemented; however the distinctions made between discipline, efficiency, hierarchy, and fellowship are not entirely clear, a shortcoming that undermines the stated goals of her study.

In her introduction Andrzejewski suggests that the intents of surveillance that she has identified are inherently different and fall outside the "context of discipline" and Foucault's understanding of surveillance and modern society. The claim to go beyond Foucault's understanding is the basis for one of the primary goals of her study. She states the following:

Foucault linked surveillance to modernity through the early-nineteenth-century prison, claiming the visual relationships at work there exemplified those that proliferated subsequently throughout modern institutions and everyday life. Although I agree with Foucault's contention that surveillance is inextricably linked with the rise of modernity, the panoptic and disciplinary manifestations he described illustrate only one aspect of surveillance. Foucault's coupling of surveillance and modernity is reconsidered and refined in the chapters

that follow through discussions about how gazes worked through different kinds of modern spaces outside the context of discipline. (6–7)

Contrary to these claims, I believe many scholars would agree that Foucault did not argue that the link between surveillance and modernity grew out of, or occurred subsequent to, the birth of the prison; rather, the prison was identified by Foucault, in the words of social theorist David Garland, "as the place where modern techniques of control are revealed in their full unbridled operation," with surveillance being one of these modern techniques.[1] The prison, and more specifically the panopticon, was not the source of the surveillance-modernity link; rather, it epitomized the forms of power and control that were at work in modern society. Furthermore, Foucault understood that his study of prisons did not capture all aspects of surveillance or other techniques of control. He said as much in a 1977 interview: "A whole history remains to be written of spaces—which would at the same time be the history of powers (both these terms in the plural)—from the great strategies of geopolitics to the little tactics of the habitat, institutional architecture from the classroom to the design of hospitals."[2]

Nevertheless, these points do not lessen the value of Andrzejewski's study; they place it more firmly within Foucault's analysis of power. Andrzejewski succeeds in her goal of adding detail to and refining Foucault's surveillance–modernity link. My reading of the work suggests that the evidence presented in her four chapters constitutes a further elaboration, not a reconsideration, of Foucault's analysis of power in modern society. Each chapter of *Building Power* reinforces discipline as a thread woven into the regulative techniques that are intended to produce a desired effect, whether it is efficiency, hierarchy, or fellowship.

In the end Andrzejewski produces a substantial contribution to the writing about space and expands prevailing understandings of what informs those who determine how spaces are designed. Perhaps more significantly, the analysis is conducted via an exploration of surveillance and the discourse that elevated its importance. Two chapters deserve further discussion: chapter 2, "Efficiency," and chapter 4, "Fellowship."

Chapter 2 is an examination of the numerous ways that surveillance was used to increase efficiency in Victorian workplaces. Andrzejewski demonstrates that while efficiency was the stated intent, it was, in fact, an intermediate goal and a means to an end that would be achieved through the creation of a disciplined and regulated workforce. As such, the chapter is also an examination of discipline. The author takes steps to distinguish work discipline from penal discipline and notes that in the case of work spaces, it is primarily meant to gain a competitive edge in the marketplace and to increase profit rather than to punish. However, discipline is an integral part of the dominant intent of efficiency. This distinction between a profit goal versus discipline as part of punishment is less important than the varied strategies that Andrzejewski reveals were used to incorporate surveillance into Victorian work spaces.

Most of the chapter is dedicated to a discussion of surveillance implemented through wholly conspicuous and open means such as raised platforms at the end of an open work space or the lack of doors on restroom stalls. However, Andrzejewski begins the chapter with the fascinating case of post office design at the end of the nineteenth century and the beginning of the twentieth century, which followed a different model. In Victorian-era post offices, a dual surveillance intent led those who determined the design of postal work spaces to use an integrated form of both conspicuous and hidden means of surveillance. Here surveillance served the dual intent of catching depredators of other people's mail and instilling worker discipline for more efficient processing. Those who controlled the design of postal work spaces employed physically prominent yet enclosed lookouts that concealed the act of surveillance, which occurred through louvered openings and peepholes. Open work spaces were also employed to facilitate both the act and feeling of surveillance. The possibility of being seen was the force that fostered self-regulation and worker discipline; the act of surveillance was the force that caught depredators and loafers. In many respects, the strategy was panoptic.

Unlike the other workplaces examined in the chapter, worker discipline and efficiency in the postal service was not aimed toward greater profits but toward meeting the challenge of a rapidly increasing amount of mail due in part to expanded service in rural areas and increased use of mail service by businesses. The desire to establish worker discipline and efficiency was also intended to build public trust in the postal service. The public needed reassurance that mail would be delivered in a timely fashion and that contents would not be stolen or destroyed. In response, the postal service aimed to create dependable delivery through the use of surveillance. As such, surveillance served a symbolic purpose as well. Andrzejewski does not highlight this point; however, her examination of post office work spaces has revealed it.

The number of examples that Andrzejewski considers in this chapter is laudable; they include textile mills, machine shops, metal-working shops, a blade shop, a stenographers' pool, a phonograph, and sanitary manufacturing companies. The surveillance strategies used in these spaces are explored through both the built environment and the discourse of industrial engineers and other prescriptive literature on the design of work spaces. Nearly all of the spaces that are examined in this chapter are located in the eastern United States, and all are situated within single buildings. The inclusion of work spaces in the West, especially from the mining and lumber industries, would have provided salient examples of surveillance strategies in more varied physical environments. An examination of these industries and others where unions were active also would have offered an opportunity to examine resistance to surveillance efforts. Nonetheless, the breadth of information and examples that Andrzejewski includes in this chapter will challenge most readers to reconsider what they understand about the strategies and manifestations of surveillance throughout the landscape of the Victorian United States.

In chapter 4, Andrzejewski examines the ways surveillance operated in what she describes as a context of fellowship. Andrzejewski argues that surveillance was intended to help strengthen social relationships between people who fraternized because of shared goals, interests, or obligations. She uses Methodist and Holiness campsites to explore surveillance for the purpose of fellowship. The author recalls the seminal work of cultural anthropologist Victor Turner and characterizes these camps located in the woods away from everyday life as liminal spaces where daily hierarchies, customs, and rules are suspended as individuals and families come together for fellowship and worship.

Surveillance in a fellowship context, according to Andrzejewski, was meant to be reciprocal and ever present. She identifies a straightforward use of spatial organization to encourage and enhance the gaze from worshippers to the minister, from the minister to worshippers, and of worshippers on one another. The spatial organization meant to support fellowship surveillance was created and promoted through both the physical environment of the camps and described in Holiness and Methodist camp literature.

Through this case study, the author illustrates, perhaps more successfully than in any other chapter in the book, how surveillance can be multidirectional and can occur on multiple levels throughout a single landscape. Andrzejewski characterizes surveillance in the context of fellowship as pervading both worship and living space throughout the camps. A centralized plan with the worship space in the center and closely spaced tents or cabins arrayed in concentric circles or along roads that radiated from the worship space, were standard. With little space between individual cabins and little or no separation between circulation pathways that led throughout the camps, and with cabin-fronts featuring large windows, even living spaces were visible to all passersby. The success that Andrzejewski achieves through a highly focused examination of the ideology and intent of camp design comes, however, at the expense of not conveying how those who attended the camp meetings used and experienced the space.

Fellowship, the singular intent of the surveillance that the author identifies in the Holiness and Methodist camps, is perhaps too narrowly defined to capture the complex realities that were likely at play within the camps. The camps were, in a sense, treated as sanctified space where sinful behavior and the temptations of everyday life were to be kept out. Although Andrzejewski never characterizes the camps as such, those who created the camps out of profane space in the woods intended for the people who came to worship to read them as sanctified space. This too informed their decisions about camp design.

The author draws upon engravings depicting the camps, site plans, Holiness and Methodist camp literature that described and prescribed how camps should be laid out, and late twentieth-century photographs of the sites. She devotes much attention to the details of nineteenth-century engravings that depict orderly rows of worshippers, all with their eyes gazing on the minister and his on them. It was easy to identify people who came as spectators rather than participants, the author tells us, because they sat near the periphery and their eyes were not on the highly visible exhorter perched on a raised platform. Andrzejewski's interpretation of the depicted

scenes seems accurate, but the image itself should be scrutinized, since it too is a product of the discourse, not a snapshot of the reality on the ground. Andrzejewski seems to miss this and a few other crucial points, leading at times to an apparent idealization of the Holiness and Methodist camps and an insufficiently critical stance toward fellowship.

The author's description of the Holiness and Methodist camps—including why worshippers attended, how individuals behaved while they were there, and the intent of those who ran the camps—is too totalizing and uniform. Did all external, everyday hierarchies really disappear? Did itinerant ministers have no intent other than to transform worshippers? Were the camps free? Could anyone attend? Were there violators of the prescribed order? How were the camps viewed by those from the outside? Did any of these factors inform those who prescribed and built these camps?

Andrzejewski's examination of surveillance within the context of fellowship would have benefited from a discussion of revivalism as well as religious expression, practices, and tolerance in the Victorian United States. Perhaps more important to the intent of the author, this chapter would have been strengthened if resistance and disobedience were discussed so that the worshippers did not read as volunteer robots controlled, transfixed, and transformed through the power of a multidirectional gaze.

Not dissimilar to the prison, the formality and rigidity of spatial definition inscribed in the camp landscapes are clearly visible; however, the practices, experiences, and actions within these spaces often escaped surveillance and control. In a 1982 interview, Foucault stated: "It is true that for me, architecture, in the very vague analysis of it that I have been able to conduct, is only taken as an element of support, to ensure a certain allocation of people in space, a canalization of their circulation, as well as the coding of their reciprocal relations."[3] I believe Andrzejewski would agree that the Holiness and Method-

ist camps achieved just this in their layout and design, and that the gaze was not always transformative, nor the obedience or fellowship so totalizing.

NOTES

1. David Garland, *Punishment and Modern Society* (Chicago: University of Chicago Press, 1990), 135.

2. Michel Foucault, *Power/Knowledge: Selected Interviews and Other Writings 1972–1977*, ed. Colin Gordon (New York: Pantheon Books, 1980), 149.

3. Paul Rabinow, ed., *The Foucault Reader* (New York: Pantheon Books, 1984), 252.

Christopher B. Leinberger
The Option of Urbanism: Investing in a New American Dream

Washington, D.C.: Island Press, 2009.
232 pages. 29 black and white illustrations.
ISBN 978-1-59726-137-1, $19.95 PB

Review by Matthew Gordon Lasner

Developers on the Verge of a New Built Environment

Since the early 1990s, metropolitan America has seen a great wave of new investment in downtown and other "urban" kinds of housing. Before the real estate market collapsed in 2007, city after city (and, increasingly, suburb after suburb), from Charleston to Detroit to Los Angeles, saw loft conversions in once-industrial neighborhoods, sleek highrise condos next to transit hubs and sports arenas, and apartment complexes atop new open-air "lifestyle center" shopping malls. What perhaps began with back-to-the-city gentrification among counterculture types in the 1960s and 1970s blossomed by the late 1990s and early 2000s into a real estate phenomenon unprecedented in postwar America: the pouring of big money into relatively high-density, multifamily housing in "walkable" locations.

Christopher B. Leinberger, a well-known

real estate consultant and occasional developer now affiliated with the Brookings Institution and the University of Michigan's graduate real estate program, has long observed this phenomenon, both professionally and as a resident of Atlanta and of Washington, D.C., places that feature prominently in *The Option of Urbanism*. He has concluded that these new genres of housing represent the leading edge of a shift in how and where most Americans want to—and eventually will—live. He argues that the American dream of a detached suburban house in what he calls a "drivable suburban" environment is being superseded by a new version of the good life: that offered by "walkable urbanism." Unfortunately, Leinberger writes, despite substantial shifts in real estate production over the past fifteen years, conservative structural forces have stifled change, leading to an oversupply of conventional suburbia. A primary goal of this book is to nudge the real estate industry in the right direction by exposing this gap between supply and demand.

The book is organized into eight chapters, along with an introduction and a preface. (The paperback edition includes an additional preface, written in late 2008 or early 2009, that responds to the current depressed real estate market; the main body of the text seems to have been completed in 2007.) Chapters 1 and 2 discuss the genesis of drivable suburbanism and outline its distinguishing features. While there is little new for historians, chapter 2 in particular offers a useful overview of the emergence of the edge city, a topic that enjoyed much attention in the 1980s and early 1990s but little since. Chapters 3 and 4 cover the logic of real estate production since the 1980s and rehearse the many familiar limits of this model of growth, from social segregation to obesity to climate change. Chapters 5, 6, and 7 outline the contours of walkable urbanism: where it is, what it looks like, who lives there, its prospects for growth, its benefits, and its potential shortcomings. In the final chapter Leinberger explores some of the tools available for stimulating the production of walkable urbanism, and encourages us to use them.

One of the most illuminating parts of *The Option of Urbanism* is the discussion, in chapter 3, of long-term changes in the way that real estate development has been financed in the United States. Before the late 1980s, Leinberger points out, most real estate development was financed locally. During the real estate boom of the 1980s, much of the money came from poorly regulated savings-and-loan-type financial institutions (S&Ls), which began engaging in fast-and-loose lending. In the wake of the real estate bust of the late 1980s and early 1990s (accompanied by the S&L crisis and bail-out), developers needed new partners. Regulators in Washington were anxious to avoid the mistakes of the past. Wall Street investment houses came forward with assurances that they would behave carefully. New partnerships were formed, and by 1993 shortages of construction credit evaporated.

The specific requirements of different sources of investment have always helped shape production of the built environment (think, for example, of the FHA and subdivision design). This particular marriage, however, changed things in unprecedented ways. With little expertise in real estate and intense pressure to see stock-market-quick returns on investment, Wall Street developed simple guidelines for different kinds of projects, from hotels and housing to office and commercial space. Projects that conformed to these standards were funded quickly and easily, while those that did not languished. An additional advantage of this system for Wall Street was that by making projects more standard, it also made them more liquid—that is, easy to sell. This situation is a major point of frustration for Leinberger, who believes that Wall Street has discouraged production of walkable urbanism because it is "baffling to build for much of the development industry due to its relative complexity" (10), and it is too slow to turn a profit.

A more general but equally unfortunate consequence, Leinberger suggests, has been standardization of the physical form of every investor-approved category of real estate (including "garden rental apartments," "move-up for-sale housing," and "big-box anchored retail"). Echoing suburban Jeremiahs like James Howard Kunstler, Leinberger writes that for the past generation, for day-to-day shopping "most of us have had the option of going to a 1980s strip mall or a 1990s strip mall . . . America provides choice galore once we get into the grocery store, but . . . only one choice in the type of environment in which we live, work, and play" (5). In other words, everything, everywhere began to look the same. In an equally evocative (if perhaps overstated) passage, he notes that only during "the last fifteen minutes of design" do architects even inquire of developers where such projects will be located. "If he is told it will be in southern California a Mediterranean tile roof and stucco will be specified. If it is to be in Washington, D.C., it will have an eighteenth-century Federalist-style brick façade with white pillars" (52). There are, of course, many other reasons that scholars have identified for the generic appearance of the American built environment—and recent debate over chain stores suggests Americans remain divided about whether regional convergence is necessarily undesirable—but this dynamic is a new and important part of the story.[1]

Students of the contemporary built environment will find much of interest in *The Option of Urbanism*. Despite sustained efforts since the 1960s by historians and architectural historians to understand how real estate development works, there remain many gaps in the literature. Much of this gap stems from the fact that developers (and the entire homebuilding apparatus, including publications of trade groups like the National Association of Real Estate Boards and the Urban Land Institute) and historians speak different professional languages. Leinberger helps to bridge this divide by making the discourse of real estate finance more transparent.

For example, one great contribution of this study is the attention given to segmentation within the real estate market. That collectors of marketing data categorize people in ever more precise ways ("White Picket Fences," "Close-in Couples") based on geographic and demographic data is not news. But there is little in the literature on the American built environment that discusses how home builders employ these categories or, more generally, how the housing landscape reflects market segmentation and, in turn, changes with demographic shifts. Simply pointing out that many Americans move to different kinds of places at different points in their lives—and that different kinds of households prefer different kinds of housing—makes a welcome addition to knowledge in the field. More specific points, such as the fact that the number of Americans turning sixty-five each year has grown from 350,000 in the early 2000s to 800,000 today and will reach 1.5 million in the mid-2010s, or that by 2025 the number of single-person households will equal the number of those with school-age children (each comprising 28 percent of the total), constitute a startling challenge to those skeptical of Leinberger's argument.

Although *The Option of Urbanism* succeeds as a primer on early twenty-first-century real estate practices, it is weaker in other areas. Central to Leinberger's argument is the idea that contemporary real estate standards are at odds with current market preferences for housing. From the mid-1990s through the mid-2000s, Wall Street financed thousands of banker-approved "entry level" and "luxury" single-family subdivisions, "build to suit" suburban office parks, and "neighborhood center" strip malls. According to Leinberger, however, what many people wanted were places where they could walk. While this discrepancy may exist, Leinberger does not offer the evidence to prove it. In lieu, he proposes that the higher price of land evident in walkable centers (relative to the drivable suburban edge) suggests market preference for it. He also cites recent housing-choice studies. These studies pair images of quaint main streets with those of generic McMansions and ask respondents

where they would ideally prefer to live. The scholarly literature has surprisingly little to say on the matter of how people specifically select where and how to live, but long-term patterns of urban change suggest that for the majority of Americans, square footage is a leading determinative factor. That such surveys focus on neighborhood rather than living space seems to undermine their value.[2]

Another limitation of the book is that Leinberger sets up, and often refers back to, a false historical dichotomy between the postwar era (visits to King of Prussia mall) and that which preceded it (Philadelphia's Market Street). Although he faults other students of the American landscape, such as Robert Bruegmann and Joel Kotkin, for using history to justify sprawl, Leinberger uses history to suggest that the drivable sub-urbanism—most of what has been built in the United States since the 1920s—is a historical anomaly, "a massive social engineering experiment" (25) with little precedent and, by extension, little future. Before World War II, he writes, Americans lived in compact communities and walked (or took public transit) nearly everywhere. But after the war, there was no option apart from drivable suburbia. This characterization is overwrought, especially given that his long-time business partner, Robert Charles Lesser, spent the 1950s and 1960s developing alternatives to single-family suburbia in the form of FHA-insured co-op apartments, a fact not discussed in the book.[3]

Equally problematic is Leinberger's insistence that the shape of the postwar built environment—along with its "market acceptance" (53) and the public policies that helped realize it—was informed primarily by Futurama, Norman Bel Geddes's tower-and-freeway diorama at General Motors' 1939 World's Fair pavilion. Although he also targets Le Corbusier (and, to a lesser degree, Walter Gropius, Ludwig Mies van der Rohe, and Frank Lloyd Wright) as the originators of modernist "neverland" urbanism, he argues repeatedly that the postwar landscape was a result of "implementation of the Futurama vision" (25). Although

he disagrees with Bruegmann and Kotkin, he might have turned to them—and, more crucially, to the work of architectural historians like Richard Longstreth and "new suburban historians" such as Greg Hise and Becky Nicolaides—for richer, more nuanced explanations for twentieth-century American urban form. As it stands, Leinberger's historiographic framework (like his endnotes) all but begins and ends with Kenneth Jackson's *Crabgrass Frontier*, published in 1985. This tendency to flatten historical complexity also characterizes his discussions of more recent decades. For example, he writes that twenty-five years ago Washington's Dupont Circle was a dangerous place that the middle class avoided, and that the only two walkable neighborhoods in the region were Georgetown and Arlington, Virginia. Both statements are gross exaggerations.

Despite his plea for more development of walkable urbanism, Leinberger does not adequately define it. Functionally it seems to include anywhere where one can walk to any sort of shop (or some undefined number of them)—or, rather, any new development where this holds true. Leinberger, after all, is less interested in cities per se than in new real estate products. (This focus is especially apparent when he writes that metropolitan Washington—which despite the popularity of Metro remains, for the most part, a driving city—has more "walkable places" than any other U.S. city, including New York, Chicago, and San Francisco!) His primary operative criterion, then, seems less to be utility than a normative vision of what "urbanism" ought to look like. One suspects that for Leinberger—as for Jane Jacobs, New Urbanists, and the millions of people who prefer to live in the walkable centers of New York, Chicago, or San Francisco—good urbanism is nineteenth-century urbanism and bad urbanism is that which accommodates the spatial logic of the car. In this respect, *The Option of Urbanism* seems to be of a part with books arguing for the redevelopment of suburbia at urban densities, such as *Retrofitting Suburbia* (2008) by Ellen Dunham-Jones and June Williamson, which, not coincidentally, is also largely informed by the example of Atlanta. Despite all the rich literature in defense of "postsuburban" places like Southern California, many urbanists, whether architects (like Dunham-Jones and Williamson) or real estate consultants, continue to see the Sunbelt city as inherently flawed.

Leinberger's thesis might also benefit from consideration of the degree to which the trends he identifies simply reflect the latest temporary requirements of the baby boomers. At every stage of life, this demographic bubble has distorted the built environment in unprecedented but rarely permanent ways. As children, boomers helped create sitcom suburbia. In the 1960s and 1970s, when they reached adulthood, production of apartments skyrocketed to levels not seen since the 1920s, and gentrification began in earnest. By the 1980s and 1990s boomers moved to suburban houses, leaving in their wake a landscape littered with aging "swinging singles" apartment complexes, which became filled with economically marginal families displaced from older areas by redevelopment projects and gentrification (a trend that continued unabated throughout this era) and, more recently, new immigrants. Little in the historical record—or in the evidence he offers, which is mainly real estate trade studies and quantitative yet descriptive demographic reports by urban planners like Arthur C. Nelson—suggests that an American dream of an apartment at the mall has replaced that of a freestanding manse. Likewise *The Option of Urbanism* excludes other kinds of arrangements that history suggests are likely to grow with the number of retirees, such as Florida condos and golf-cart subdivisions like Leisure World.

Leinberger's point that Americans should have more choice in how and where to live is unquestionably correct, although it remains to be seen whether many families care to give up large houses or, more crucially, their cars for day-to-day errands. Whether or not his thesis holds, *The Option of Urbanism* offers a compelling map of the real estate industry today. Gaps remain. But for those of us interested in understanding the shape and direction of building production in the millennial metropolis, it is a good place to begin.

NOTES

1. On the generic appearance of buildings in the United States, see Larry Ford, *Cities and Buildings: Skyscrapers, Skid Rows, and Suburbs* (Baltimore: The Johns Hopkins University Press, 1994); Margaret Crawford, "The World in a Shopping Mall," in *Variations on a Theme Park: The New American City and the End of Public Space*, ed. Michael Sorkin, 3–30 (New York: Hill and Wang, 1992); John Chase, "The Role of Consumerism in American Architecture," *Journal of Architectural Education* 44, no. 4 (August 1991): 211–24; Carol Willis, *Form Follows Finance: Skyscrapers and Skylines in New York and Chicago* (New York: Princeton Architectural Press, 1995); Philip Langdon, *Orange Roofs, Golden Arches: The Architecture of American Chain Restaurants* (New York: Knopf, 1986); Chester H. Leibs, *Main Street to Miracle Mile: American Roadside Architecture* (Boston: Little, Brown, 1985).

On recent debate over the chain store, see Virginia Postrel, "In Praise of Chain Stores," *The Atlantic*, December 2006; Daniel Scroop, "The Anti-Chain Store Movement and the Politics of Consumption," *American Quarterly* 60, no. 4 (December 2008): 925–49; Richard Longstreth, "Bringing 'Downtown' to the Neighborhoods: Wieboldt's, Goldblatt's, and the Creation of Department Store Chains in Chicago," *Buildings & Landscapes* 14 (2007): 13–49; Robert Spector, *Category Killers: The Retail Revolution and Its Impact on Consumer Culture* (Boston: Harvard Business Press, 2005).

2. Scholars (primarily social scientists) have long studied housing preferences, but using broad categories, such as tenure (owning, renting), neighborhood racial composition, physical typology (house, apartment), school quality, and general geography (city, suburb). For a recent example of this kind of work, see Arthur C. Nelson, "The New Urbanity: The Rise of a New America," *The Annals of the American Academy of Political and Social Science* 626 (2009): 192–208.

On the absence in the scholarly literature of finer-grained approaches to this question, see David Steigerwald, "All Hail the Republic of Choice: Consumer History as Contemporary Thought," *Journal of American History* 93, no. 2 (September 2006): 385–403; Richard White, "Sprawl: The View from Toronto," *Journal of Planning History* 8, no. 3 (August 2009): 274–83 at 280; Robert Bruegmann, *Sprawl: A Compact History* (Chicago: University of Chicago Press, 2005).

3. Matthew Gordon Lasner, "Own-your-owns, Co-ops, Town Houses: Hybrid Housing Types and the New Urban Form in Postwar Southern California," *Journal of the Society of Architectural Historians* 68, no. 3 (September 2009): 378–403.

Cynthia Falk
Architecture and Artifacts of the Pennsylvania Germans: Constructing Identity in Early America

University Park: Pennsylvania State University Press, 2008. 256 pages. 108 black-and-white photographs and plans, appendices.
ISBN 978-0-271-03338-9, $45.00 HB

Review by Sally McMurry

This beautifully produced volume carries on a distinguished tradition of scholarship about buildings produced by a well-known early American social group, the Pennsylvania Germans. Cynthia Falk's fine study combines conventional historical analysis with careful readings of material objects to produce a thoughtful reinterpretation of familiar architectural monuments.

Most of the buildings analyzed here, such as the Zeller house, the Peter Wentz house, and the Miller's house at Millbach are iconic monuments for American architectural historians and students of colonial material culture. Falk's contribution does not substantially expand the universe of documented buildings (though new documentation of the Eshleman house in Lancaster County is presented); its purpose is to offer fresh perspectives on interpreting them. Her central claim is that historians have been too quick to see the buildings as expressions of ethnicity, to the exclusion of other factors that were historically more important. In five richly illustrated chapters, she develops alternative interpretations with the goal of understanding "the meanings ascribed to buildings and belongings in late eighteenth-century Pennsylvania," and more particularly "how objects served as expressions of identity." In doing so, she makes a contribution to an area already established as crucial by leading scholars such as T. H. Breen and Laurel Thatcher Ulrich (2).

The first chapter, "German or Georgian?" follows on previous scholarship, both utilizing earlier insights and offering new ones. Early investigators tended to "essentialize" what they saw as "pure" Pennsylvania German expression. They focused on the so-called Continental house as the quintessentially Pennsylvania German house. This form was a (usually) three-room house with center chimney, long entry kitchen (küche), "stove-room" (stube) heated by a five-plate stove fed from the kitchen hearth, and unheated or bedroom chamber (kammer). As Falk notes, however, William Woys Weaver and Charles Bergengren have brought new evidence to bear that complicates Pennsylvania Germans' relationships with these forms. Indisputably, the form is clearly associated with Pennsylvania settlers from German-speaking Europe; but Weaver has found that the so called Continental house was not very common at all in Europe, and indeed may have been developed most fully in Pennsylvania, while Bergengren finds several other types associated with German-speaking residents.

Falk acknowledges their findings but offers a different interpretive perspective. Most important, she takes issue with their assumption that artifacts that display definite and identifiable cultural practices necessarily were expressions of ethnicity. An important contextual point that she makes is that the Pennsylvania German population was itself far from homogeneous; it was divided by class

and religion, to name two of the more important social fault lines. Thus, she maintains, to argue for a cohesive Pennsylvania German ethnic expression is a mistake. Her argument is further developed as she takes up a building form that was new after the mid-eighteenth century. The form commonly labeled German-Georgian combines architectural traits clearly connected to German Pennsylvanians' cultural practices (for example, retaining stoves, or conversely using the term "stove room" for a room heated by a fireplace) with the symmetry, closed center-passage floor plan, and classical trim characteristic of the late colonial architectural style we call Georgian. Falk takes issue with the very opposition the question poses, with the notion that just because a building combines architectural repertoires that it is somehow "schizophrenic." She argues that such combinations are evidence not of ambivalence or assimilation (a claim made by several other scholars), but rather that they represent owners' aspirations to gentility; their creators saw no contradiction in wanting to have the latest ornament while also retaining some features carried along from their repertoire of German-derived cultural practices. Falk maintains that these later houses embody what Cary Carson has suggested is a choice between folk and formal rather than between German and English.[1]

Falk's arguments rest primarily on presenting an alternative way of reading the buildings and on a different imagining of their architectural features than has usually been the case. Read in this way, the buildings do take on a new significance. Yet much of the power of Falk's interpretation derives from the altered point of view rather than from original architectural analysis. The features she points out—for example, symmetry, stove rooms, construction features, and layout—have been noted by others. Her contribution is to see new meaning in the assemblage.

In the second chapter, "Industry, Economy, and Ignorance," Falk explores outsiders' perceptions of Pennsylvania German material life. Some were more or less objective;

for example, almost all observers connected Pennsylvania Germans to cultural practices of using heating stoves, preferring bright color, following specific foodways, building houses over springs, and the like. Yet Falk notes that in other respects, non–Pennsylvania Germans' observations almost willfully ignored objective reality. Falk persuasively shows, using Direct Tax data, that the material culture–based stereotypes do not hold at all: elite Pennsylvania Germans' houses hardly differed in value or size from those built by others. Outsiders *saw* differences because they wanted to further certain agendas. A case in point is their assessment of Pennsylvania Germans as agrarians. Some disparaged the Pennsylvania Germans' alleged tendency to have large barns and poorly built houses, which they then connected to ignorance and crudeness. Conversely, other observers lauded the Pennsylvania Germans' supposed superior agrarian practices as best for a republic while still perceiving a lack of sophistication in Pennsylvania German life, which they saw as virtuous simplicity. Both agreed on the contours of Pennsylvania German life but interpreted them differently. Falk places outsiders' stereotypes within the larger context of debates over the direction of the new republic as they pondered whether the United States should stress a commercial or an agrarian future. She asserts that it is a mistake for contemporary scholars to take them at face value. This is a valuable corrective to so much scholarship that has tended to do just that.

In her third chapter, "From Awkwardness to Civility," Falk argues for a Pennsylvania German connection to a "multiethnic community" via architectural refinement and elites' assertion of class and economic status. Along with elites generally, Pennsylvanians of German descent chose from fashionable trends in stonemasonry, interior finish, and symmetry. They participated in the intellectual trends of the day: in the new republic, citizens linked architectural graces to social graces, to leadership, and even to morality. Improvement became the watchword. Falk dissects the debate over the Direct Tax in light of these ideas—by 1798 an argument could be made that at the high end of the housing spectrum, dwellings represented not mere necessity but a degree of status and luxury, and therefore that a progressive tax was fair. Another facet of "improvement" involved new six- and ten-plate freestanding stoves, which freed stoves from having to be tethered to a kitchen hearth and therefore resulted in repositioning many kitchens away from the ceremonial center of the house and making it easier to construct a socially closed plan. A central point here is that Pennsylvania Germans made architectural choices based as much on class as on ethnicity—that they could use buildings to project "multiple identities" (112). This is an important and innovative frame in which to see these buildings.

In the fourth chapter, "Luxury," Falk finds a "common visual language of piety" in buildings and artifacts. She explores how "identity making" is shaped not only by individuals but by communities—in this case religious or civic ones. Several important points emerge here. First, architectural expressions of religion were clearest at the extremes of the religious spectrum; she places the ascetic Ephrata Cloister and the cosmopolitan Moravians at opposite ends. Second, although there was much public discussion of things like personal behavior, morality, and piety, religious expression in architecture was clearest in meetinghouses and churches and less evident in houses. Finally, she cautions against the dangers of a "presentist" perspective that assumes that contemporary Plain Sect ideologies can be read straight back into the eighteenth century; grand houses like that of Mennonite Benedict Eshleman assertively challenge that assumption. Again she uses the Direct Tax to good effect in showing that Mennonites, Lutherans, and others whose religious affiliation can be determined were well represented among owners of grand houses. Falk makes a valuable contribution in her effort to temper one-dimensional and

perhaps ahistorical notions of "status" with more clearly eighteenth-century notions of morality and piety, even if it is sometimes hard to provide concrete connections.

The last chapter, "Changes and Choices," argues that class and wealth began to replace religion and national origin as measures of identity in the late eighteenth century because in the new republic the contours of society and economy were matters of intense concern. According to Falk, this new trend, and not a monumental shift from a premodern to a modern worldview (as advanced, for instance, in work by Charles Bergengren, James Deetz, and Henry Glassie), accounts for architectural changes of the day. Falk prefers the notion of "creolization," as advanced for example by Gabrielle Lanier—not in the sense of assimilation but of a more or less equal cultural exchange.[2] She concludes with some reflections on the implications of new perspectives for museums and other present-day interpreters.

Overall, the study is an important corrective to assumptions too long unchallenged. The book's themes tend to be interwoven rather than clearly demarcated, leading to some repetition and occasional confusion, yet the overall effect is still strong. Falk subtly differentiates specific practices, which can be clearly connected to Pennsylvania German people, from historians' interpretations of those practices, which have tended to essentialize and to ignore context. For whatever reason, this tendency is more than usually common among scholars of Pennsylvania German life.

At the same time, Falk's contentions raise questions too. Surely it is persuasive to point out that identity is multifaceted and contingent. Yet does today's preoccupation with individual identity itself—not to mention the bedrock of our materialistic culture, the assumption that our things express ourselves—pose a danger of ahistorical presentism? The notions of identity and self, not to mention individualism, are arguably modern preoccupations. How then do the very

ideas of self and identity relate to eighteenth-century architectural expression? Falk's inclusion of ideas like piety and morality are a tantalizing beginning but leave the reader looking for more.

Falk has made a significant contribution by placing these iconic buildings within a larger architectural context. For instance, through data from the Direct Tax manuscripts, she shows how elite Pennsylvania Germans' houses stood in relation to others' houses, usually in a given township. Yet two things might have made the analysis still richer, though to be sure they would have been quite challenging to document. First, a more immediate context might also be revealing. That would be the complex of domestic outbuildings, perhaps even including ancillary houses. Were these grand houses "saying" something to an audience besides the public—that is, to family and workers? If so, what might that have been? In other words, we might accept the premise that these buildings are an expressive medium and wonder if they express something beyond personal identity—a vision of social hierarchy, perhaps, or a reconceptualization of work and production. A second direction would be an attempt to find one or two architectural expressions of more "middling" members of both German-derived and other social sets in order to see what sorts of comparisons are there. For those at the top, elite status probably *did* shape their daily expressions; but what about the far more numerous "middling sort"?

Finally, the study's chronology actually ends at a point that historian Steven Nolt considers a beginning for a self-conscious collective Pennsylvania German group identity. In *Foreigners in Their Own Land: Pennsylvania Germans in the Early Republic* (2002), Nolt maintains that Pennsylvania German group identity actually first developed in the early nineteenth century and was not solidified until about 1850. Falk, by contrast, asserts that issues of national origin became less important (though not unimportant) by the early nineteenth century in public discourse, being "overshadowed by those grounded in social and economic status" (172). Of course, early nineteenth-century Pennsylvania German group consciousness may not have been expressed architecturally, but by confining herself to the eighteenth century, Falk misses an opportunity to find out what happened once Pennsylvania Germans actually thought of themselves as such.

These comments in no way diminish Falk's accomplishment. She has said something new about a corpus of buildings we thought we understood, and she has provided a firm foundation for further inquiry.

NOTES

1. T. H. Breen, *The Marketplace of the Revolution: How Consumer Politics Shaped American Independence* (New York: Oxford University Press, 2004); Laurel Thatcher Ulrich, *The Age of Homespun: Objects and Stories in the Creation of an American Myth* (New York: Knopf, 2001).

2. Charles Bergengren, "The Cycle of Transformation in the Houses of Schaefferstown, Pennsylvania." PhD diss., Folklore, University of Pennsylvania, 1988; James Deetz, *In Small Things Forgotten: The Archaeology of Early American Life* (Garden City, N.Y.: Anchor Doubleday, 1977); Henry Glassie, "Eighteenth-Century Cultural Process in Delaware Valley Folk Building," *Winterthur Portfolio* 7 (1972): 29–57.

Mary Ellen Hayward
Baltimore's Alley Houses: Homes for Working People since the 1780s

Baltimore: The Johns Hopkins University Press, 2008.
328 pages. 98 halftone illustrations, 6 line drawings.
ISBN 978-0-8018-8834-2, $45.00 HB

Review by Laura B. Driemeyer

The rowhouse likely comes to mind when one thinks about the nineteenth-century American urban residential landscape, especially in the mid-Atlantic and New England regions. The versatility of this housing form led to its widespread construction in a range of scales and styles suitable for a variety of economic classes, from laborers to the elite. Remarkably, this common building type, especially the humble variants constructed for working people, remains a relatively understudied component of the urban vernacular landscape. *Baltimore's Alley Houses: Homes for Working People since the 1780s* helps rectify this lacuna. Hayward's case study analyzes the prevalent alley house, the smallest scale of row housing in Baltimore, Maryland, "to shed light on the subject of planned housing for the poor and working classes by closely investigating the housing patterns and urban growth of one of America's most important early nineteenth-century cities" (8). This focus on small-scale row housing, constructed on narrow, mid-block alleys and built for and occupied by large numbers of the city's working people, distinguishes this volume as a valuable addition to the small but growing body of case studies of urban vernacular residential forms. The book has garnered a number of awards, including the Vernacular Architecture Forum's 2009 Abbott Lowell Cummings Prize and a 2009 Heritage Book Award given by the Maryland Historic Trust.

Baltimore's Alley Houses, a well-illustrated architectural and social history, combines fieldwork and extensive documentary research in the best tradition of vernacular architecture studies to analyze construction and residency patterns of alley houses built in the city from the late eighteenth century to about 1909, when Baltimore's new building code banned construction of new tenements and apartments on streets measuring less than forty feet in width as part of local housing reform efforts. While the rowhouse is not unique to Baltimore, as the author notes in the introduction, what distinguishes the city's row housing is the sheer quantity of examples constructed throughout the nineteenth century and the diversity of scale. Of particular significance is the large number of alley houses or small row-houses still extant. Smaller numbers of alley houses survive and were constructed in more discrete time periods in other mid-Atlantic cities: in Philadelphia alley house construction largely disappeared after the Civil War, and in Washington, DC, the form was popularized predominantly only after the Civil War (9).

This study of Baltimore's alley houses "derives from a preservation imperative" (ix) in response to the city housing commissioner's mid-1990s threat to demolish them wholesale as a means of solving the vacant housing crisis. In response to this threat, "several hundred blocks of houses" were "recorded, documented, photographed, and put on file" by local preservationists over a five-year period (ix). Hayward's book is the published end product of the analysis of the results of that heroic endeavor. That fieldwork established a baseline definition of alley houses based on location, scale, and degree of ornament. A hierarchy of rowhousing by location exists within each city block, based on street widths and their relationship to the block. Whereas developers constructed the widest three-story, three-bay rowhouses on the primary streets and slightly narrower ones on mid-block streets, on alley streets they constructed two-story, two-bay rowhouses. Alley houses front on mid-block alleys or lanes measuring less than thirty feet. Their decorative detailing tends to be a simplified or economical version of the current style at the time of their construction. The interior plan is typically two rooms deep, sometimes with a rear kitchen addition or service ell.

Baltimore's Alley Houses includes an introduction, six chapters, and an epilogue. The volume features a generous use of images including plans and elevations; historic and recent photographs; historic prints and drawings; and details from historic maps, atlases, and bird's-eye views. A double-leaf overview map at the beginning covers the sections of Baltimore discussed throughout the book, with particular sites mentioned in the text identified to help orient the reader. The introduction briefly discusses historic urban plans and rowhouses of English and colonial American cities, arguing that the Baltimore rowhouse and the method of land tenure in that city derive from English sources. In a largely chronological fashion, each subsequent chapter focuses on a specific nineteenth-century immigrant group, the local economy of that period and that group's role in it, the development of the section of Baltimore the group tended to settle in, the alley houses these working people lived in (and often owned), and the builders and developers of the blocks. Chapters generally begin and end with a story of one individual and their relationship to the section of Baltimore under discussion. This framework not only details the chronological development of the city but also the changing character of the alley rowhouse. The chapter organization works better in some instances than others.

In classic vernacular architecture studies fashion, documented buildings, primary sources (including land records, city directories, census records, payroll records, and newspapers), and secondary sources provide the evidence to analyze and interpret the changing form and use of the alley house and its patterns of construction and use. An extensive examination of land records supplies the chronologies and methods of development for different parts of the city over the course of the nineteenth century. Hayward correlates these identified chronologies with the buildings constructed in those areas to identify "patterns of stylistic influence and building development" (9–10). This information identifies the individuals "who created the look and form of the city during different periods" (10). The use of other primary documentary materials, most notably a compilation of city directory listings and census records, supplement the land records evidence to establish patterns of occupancy in the alley houses over time. Another key body of primary documentation effectively employed for this analysis is surviving payroll records for the Baltimore and Ohio Railroad Company. From these records

Hayward is able to link specific individuals with their ability to purchase a particular scale of rowhousing. The use of this impressive range of documents represents the author's long-time study of Baltimore, and the Baltimore rowhouse in particular, and a fruitful mining of primary resources.[1]

A central theme of *Baltimore's Alley Houses* is patterns of speculative development, construction financing, and how so many working people in Baltimore were able to purchase their homes (in contrast with the situation in other cities). A key premise is that the particular conditions present in Baltimore, notably the ground rent system and the methods of land development, "led to one of the largest homeownership ratios in the country by the late nineteenth century. Market driven, it reaped satisfactory profits for developers while still providing laboring people, many of whom were recent immigrants, with decent living conditions and a chance to improve their situation in the world" (9). Baltimore and Philadelphia are unusual in that they are the only two cities in America to adopt and maintain an English system of land ownership that continues to the present day. The ground rent system distributes costs while also increasing the means of income for the different parties involved in the development and ownership of newly constructed houses. The land lease system fostered full development of land in order to increase the amount of income and guaranteed a continuing source of income from the lease(s) for the landowner. In its most basic and common configuration in Baltimore, the landowner leased the property to a developer or builder, usually for ninety-nine years.[2] When constructing new housing, the developer or builder only had to cover the cost of the lease and the construction costs, which he typically recouped with the sale of the building and transfer of the lease to the new building owner. In turn, because of reduced initial costs, the builder or developer was able to develop rows of houses rather than single houses. Finally, for the new owner, acquisition of a new home involved paying for the building's sale price

and the land lease, and not any land acquisition costs.

In *Baltimore's Alley Houses,* the six chapters incorporate social, economic, immigration, and architectural history as they chart the ever-expanding nineteenth-century city of Baltimore. The first chapter examines the free African American community in the Fells Point area along the waterfront in the late eighteenth and early nineteenth century, using Frederick Douglass's story as the entrée into the neighborhood. Activities along the waterfront such as shipping and shipbuilding were the primary economic engine for this thriving and integrated area of Baltimore. In this period, the two-and-one-half-story, gable-roofed rowhouse, with dormers at the garret level, became the predominant alley house form. The buildings employed a modicum of Federal style detailing.

The settlement of the Irish in West Baltimore in the vicinity of the rapidly expanding facilities of the Baltimore and Ohio Railroad is the focus of the second chapter. This is one of the richer chapters, not only in recounting the causes of Irish emigration but also in documenting the large numbers of Irish employed by the railroad and the correlation between wages and scale of housing owned and/or occupied by specific individuals. The analysis of the alley house building in this period is more in-depth than in some of the other chapters, with a detailed description of a new small rowhouse variant, the two-story-and-attic house. This new variant for working-men, established by the 1840s, featured a low-pitched gable roof and a low-height third story with narrow, horizontal three-light windows. A minimal amount of Greek style detailing was employed on these buildings, concentrated primarily around the entry door.

The third chapter tells the story of Germans in Baltimore. While Germans had immigrated to the Baltimore area since the late eighteenth century, a significant influx overlapped with the Irish in the 1840s. The discussion concentrates, however, on the post–Civil War period and the number of

German builders active at that time; some of this material overlaps with that presented in *The Baltimore Rowhouse,* so this is not entirely new information. These German builders constructed all scales of housing, including alley houses, which by the 1870s had been modified yet again to two stories under a flat roof with wooden cornices and Italianate detailing. Hayward's analysis also touches on funding sources for these builders, notably German banks and their relationship to neighborhood building and loan associations. Such building and loan associations are a major thread in the second half of this work, and though not unique to Baltimore, their presence, combined with the ground rent system, bolster the author's argument for the high incidence of ownership in that city. These associations were important in many of the immigrant communities in the second half of the nineteenth century and well into the twentieth century because they enabled so many people to buy their own homes.

Whereas Irish and German immigrant stories in America are well documented, less so are those of Bohemian immigrants, who are the focus of the fourth chapter. This group began arriving in Baltimore in the post–Civil War period in the wake of the Austro–Prussian War that devastated their homeland. Hayward's discussion emphasizes specific Bohemian builders and the importance of building and loan associations to these newcomers. The economy of construction allowed builders to erect greater numbers of buildings at once, sometimes covering an entire half block with differently scaled rowhouses depending on their location within the block (164). By the end of the nineteenth century the alley house form remained a two-story, flat-roofed variant but now had sheet metal cornices. A key piece of primary documentation used in this chapter is the remarkable collection of photographs taken by the young Bohemian immigrant John Dubas in the early twentieth century, which is now housed at the Maryland Historical Society. The photographs include views of Dubas' Bohemian neighbors, posed outside and inside their houses and stores. Hayward uses these photographs not only to illustrate but also to analyze Bohemian-constructed, -owned, and -occupied buildings.

Hayward returns to African American neighborhoods in the fifth chapter. By the time of the Civil War, "Baltimore had the largest free black population of any American city" (181). As in the second chapter, the detailed analysis of city directory and census records documents their occupations, household sizes, and on what parts of the block they tended to live. The chapter also addresses the tensions that arose with the influx of a "much less privileged class of black citizens, former plantation slaves who had little education and few urban skills" (181). The discussion emphasizes the occupancy of older housing stock, including alley houses, as opposed to the construction of new stock, setting the stage for the following chapter.

The genesis of the documentation of Baltimore's alley houses brings us back to preservation in the last chapter. Chapter 6 distinguishes this volume from other case studies of house types, and while the content is local the implications resonate regionally and nationally. After beginning with an overly long review of reform efforts and tenements in New York City, Hayward considers reform in the City of Baltimore in the early 1900s, detailing a 1906 study of tenement house districts. This discussion is followed by a chronicling of 1930s housing that identified areas of blight that were in need of redevelopment to improve the city's tax base. This situation ultimately led to the construction of the city's first three-story, low-rental public housing blocks, which replaced large numbers of the alley houses and other row housing and frequently displaced large numbers of African Americans. The final phase of these renewal efforts, which resulted in more wholesale demolition of blocks of rowhousing, was the construction of multi-story towers for public housing. In the mid-1990s, after acknowledgment of the utter failure of that housing form, the towers were demolished to make way for the construction of low-rise housing. This final chapter deftly shows that these urban renewal efforts were extremely shortsighted and removed a great deal of small-scale, affordable housing (though admittedly lacking in modern conveniences). The displacement of the occupants of much of this housing, including alley houses, had lasting ramifications. The chapter ends in the 1970s, after the beginning of early preservation efforts (in the wake of the implementation of the National Register program in the 1960s) to reclaim and restore alley houses in Old Town, Fells Point, and Federal Hill.

The epilogue highlights the renewal and continued occupancy of the alley houses, now with technological upgrades. "In some areas of the city, the alley houses built in the nineteenth century still serve as affordable homes for working-class people or newly arrived immigrants" (262–63). In other words, the alley house endures as a viable form of housing, much as it did in the nineteenth century.

With the acknowledgment that this work is more descriptive than interpretive, the criticisms of this work are comparatively minor with two caveats. First, the wealth of detail—about particular buildings, of multiple individuals, on specific streets—can be overwhelming at times. More summary statements about building dimensions, household composition, residency by street and block, financing methods, and developers' activities would have enhanced the readability of this work; the particulars could have gone into the footnotes. This in turn would have tightened the descriptions and taken the burden off the reader to sum up patterns from material scattered throughout the text. Second, greater discussion of interior finishes, plans, and spatial usage (including service spaces like kitchens in rear ells and basements) would have enhanced the discussion immeasurably. A number of buildings illustrated in the volume sit on high foundations, but the absence of discussion of this feature and how it affects the interior plan leaves the reader to wonder how this raised basement space was used.

Certainly in other urban areas there is precedence across all scales of housing for placing the kitchen in the basement. In addition, while the builders used a hierarchy of standardized plans and finish details, did the residents use the spaces as intended? Were there tensions between the standardized plan of the builder-developers and how the residents used them?

In the end, these concerns do not diminish the otherwise rich documentation and analysis of the builders, developers, owners, and occupants presented in *Baltimore's Alley Houses*. This work will be of interest to any student of Baltimore's development and historic resources, and most particularly the alley houses constructed for and occupied by working people for nearly a century.

NOTES

1. *Baltimore's Alley Houses* both builds upon but also occasionally duplicates information in two earlier publications on the Baltimore rowhouses authored or co-authored by Hayward. They are Mary Ellen Hayward, "Urban Vernacular Architecture in Nineteenth-century Baltimore," *Winterthur Portfolio* 16, no. 1 (Spring 1981): 33–63 and Mary Ellen Hayward and Charles Belfoure, *The Baltimore Rowhouse* (New York: Princeton Architectural Press, 1999). Hayward is also the coeditor, with Frank R. Shivers Jr., of *The Architecture of Baltimore: An Illustrated History* (Baltimore: The Johns Hopkins University Press, 2004).

2. This differs somewhat from Philadelphia in that title to the lot was granted in perpetuity, subject to annual rent. Donna J. Rilling, *Making Houses, Crafting Capitalism: Builders in Philadelphia, 1790–1850* (Philadelphia: University of Pennsylvania Press, 2001), 8. See also chapter 2 in Rilling. The Baltimore system is explained in greater detail in Hayward and Belfoure, *The Baltimore Rowhouse*, 12–15.

Contributors

Annmarie Adams is William C. Macdonald professor and associate director at the School of Architecture, McGill University. She is author of *Architecture in the Family Way: Doctors, Houses, and Women, 1870–1900* and *Medicine by Design: The Architect and the Modern Hospital, 1893–1943* (Minnesota, 2008), and coauthor of *Designing Women: Gender and the Architectural Profession.*

Butte native **Edwin Dobb** is a fourth-generation descendant of Cornish tin miners and Irish copper miners. A former editor of *The Sciences,* Dobb writes for *National Geographic, Harper's,* and *The New York Times Magazine,* among other publications. Dobb is cowriter and coproducer of the feature-length documentary *Butte, America.* He is lecturer at the University of California–Berkeley Graduate School of Journalism and is an adjunct professor in the Environmental Studies Program at the University of Montana, Missoula.

Laura B. Driemeyer is an architectural historian for Preservation Company, a preservation consulting firm in Kensington, New Hampshire. She holds a PhD in American and New England studies from Boston University, where her dissertation, "Rising from the Ashes: The Transformation of Nineteenth-Century Building Culture in Charlestown, Massachusetts," examined the actions of several generations of Charlestown building craftsmen as they engaged with the socioeconomic changes in the period 1789–1873, and the urban vernacular house forms they constructed. She coauthored volume 3 of *The Early Architecture and Landscapes of the Narragansett Basin.*

Elaine Jackson-Retondo is a historian in the National Park Service, Pacific West Regional Office. Originally from Johnstown, Pennsylvania, she earned her doctorate in architectural history from the University of California–Berkeley in 2001. She resides in Oakland, California.

Matthew Gordon Lasner is assistant professor of history at Georgia State University in Atlanta. He studies the history and theory of the built environment, with primary focus on urban and suburban form in the late nineteenth- and twentieth-century United States. His current research concerns the history of condo living in metropolitan America, in particular the emergence, between the 1880s and 1970s, of owner-occupied, multifamily housing as an alternative to the single-family subdivision. He earned his PhD at Harvard in 2007.

Lillian Makeda is an architectural historian living in Gallup, New Mexico, where she researches, teaches, and writes about the cultural landscape of the Four Corners region. She was recently the recipient of a research fellowship from the State of New Mexico to study soil conservation service projects on the Navajo reservation. Her historic preservation work is currently focused on Mormon trading posts and New Deal–era Navajo schools.

Sally McMurry is a professor of history at Penn State University. She is author of *From Sugar Camps to Star Barns*; *Transforming Rural Life*; and *Families and Farmhouses in Nineteenth-Century America*. She is working on a field guide to Pennsylvania's historic barns and outbuildings.

Allen S. Miller teaches American and world history at Lancaster Country Day School in Lancaster, Pennsylvania. He received his master's degree in American history, focusing on state building and technology in the early American republic, from the University of Virginia in 2007. Previously he had worked in the software industry for more than twenty-five years.

Travis E. Nygard is a PhD candidate at the University of Pittsburgh in the Department of the History of Art and Architecture. His dissertation, "Seeds of Agribusiness: Grant Wood and the Visual Culture of Grain Farming, 1862–1957," argues that the large-scale, vertically integrated, transnational, scientifically intensive, and corporate-controlled farming of the twenty-first century came to be accepted through visual materials during an earlier era.

Pamela H. Simpson is the Ernest Williams II Professor of Art History at Washington and Lee University, where she has taught since 1973. Her books include *The Architecture of Historic Lexington* (coauthored with Royster Lyle), *Cheap, Quick, and Easy: Imitative Architectural Materials, 1870–1930*, and *Monuments to the Lost Cause: Women, Art, and the Landscapes of Southern Memory* (coedited with Cindy Mills). A founding member of Vernacular Architecture Forum, she has served as president, board member, and editor of the *Perspectives in Vernacular Architecture* journal. She is working on a book on corn palaces and butter sculpture.

Join the Vernacular Architecture Forum

Please enroll me as a member of the Vernacular Architecture Forum. I understand that membership entitles me to the next two issues of the biannual journal *Buildings & Landscapes: Journal of the Vernacular Architecture Forum* and the next four issues of the quarterly *Vernacular Architecture Newsletter (VAN)*, and that my subscription will begin with the next issue of the newsletter after the receipt of my dues. Membership also includes optional enrollment in our members e-mail list, and members receive advance notice of VAF conferences and tours.

Membership Categories

☐ Active, $60*   ☐ Multiyear Active, _____ x $60*

☐ Household, $80* (includes one copy of publications per household)

☐ Student, $30* (Name of School: _____)

☐ Institution, $90*   ☐ Contributing, $90**

☐ Patron, $165**   ☐ Lifetime, $2,000** (Payable in four $500 installments over a four-year period)

Membership Outside North America

☐ Add $5 to above categories, other than Lifetime, for postage

Enrollment Information

_____
NAME(S)

_____
ADDRESS

_____
CITY   STATE/PROVINCE   ZIP

_____
COUNTRY

_____
E-MAIL (IF YOU WISH TO JOIN OUR MEMBERS E-MAIL LIST)   TELEPHONE

Note: Memberships must be paid by check or money order in U.S. funds. VAF does not currently accept credit cards. Make checks payable to VAF and mail to: Gabrielle M. Lanier, Secretary
Vernacular Architecture Forum
P.O. Box 1511
Harrisonburg, VA 22803-1511

_____

*Active, Household, Institution, and Student Members: Please consider an additional gift in support of VAF programs.

$ _____ Student and Professional Support Fund (including grants, fellowships, and awards)

$ _____ Publications Fund (including *Buildings & Landscapes*, *VAN*, and special publications)

$ _____ VAF Endowment Fund

**Contributing, Patron, and Lifetime Members: All receipts above the basic $60 active membership category will be applied toward the giving category or categories of your choice (please check one or more):

☐ Student and Professional Support Fund

☐ Publications Fund

☐   VAF Endowment Fund

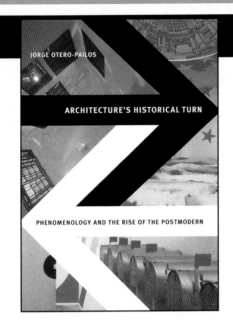